6⁰⁰

BLACK
to the
GRINDSTONE

Also by Arthur Black

Basic Black (1981)
Back to Black (1987)
That Old Black Magic (1989)
Arthur! Arthur! (1991)
Black by Popular Demand (1993)
Black in the Saddle Again (1996)
Black Tie and Tales (1999)
Flash Black (2002)
Black & White and Read All Over (2004)
Pitch Black (2005)
Black Gold (2006)

BLACK
to the
GRINDSTONE

ARTHUR BLACK

HARBOUR PUBLISHING

Harbour Publishing Co. Ltd.
P.O. Box 219
Madeira Park, BC
V0N 2H0
www.harbourpublishing.com

Cover photograph: Howard Fry
Printed in Canada

Harbour Publishing acknowledges financial support from the Government of Canada through the Book Publishing Industry Development Program and the Canada Councilfor the Arts, and from the Province of British Columbia through the British Columbia Arts Council and the Book Publisher's Tax Credit.

THE CANADA COUNCIL | LE CONSEIL DES ARTS
FOR THE ARTS | DU CANADA
SINCE 1957 | DEPUIS 1957

BRITISH
COLUMBIA
ARTS COUNCIL
Supported by the Province of British Columbia

Library and Archives Canada Cataloguing in Publication

Black, Arthur
    Black to the grindstone / Arthur Black.

ISBN 978-1-55017-442-7

    1. Canadian wit and humor (English) I. Title.

PS8553.L318B527 2007   C818'.5402   C2007-903913-8

Contents

ANIMAL, MINERAL, VEGETABLE

Those Revolting Animals — 11

Slippery Jack and the Shameless Stinkhorn — 14

Clearing the Deck — 17

Only Connect — 20

A-Hunting We Won't Go — 23

You Say Tomato, I Say Yuck — 26

The Dog Days of Winter — 29

How Does Your Garden Grow? — 32

Cow Tipping: the Udder Truth — 35

Fritz the Cinema Cat — 38

CHAOS THEORY

Live More, Work Less — 43

The Camera Doesn't Lie . . . Sometimes — 46

The Law is an Ass — 49

Nice Work If You Can Get It — 52

Liberal: Just a Four-Letter Word — 55

Lawsuits to Die For — 58

Counting Our Blessings — 61

Bonehead Bureaucratic Blunders — 64

School Boards: Thick as Planks — 67

I'll Sue You in My Dreams — 70

Of All the Gaul! — 73

Generalissimo Franco is Still Dead — 76

BODY LANGUAGE

Have a Nice Day — 81

Hey, Big Guy, Got a Macho? — 84

Hands Off My Hands — 87

Laugh? I Thought I'd Diet — 90

Too Dumb to Live — 93

The Shoes We Choose . . .   *96*

Take It Off, Eh?   *99*

Should You Smoke After Sex?   *102*

Beauty is Only Scalpel Deep   *105*

My Back Story   *108*

Fancy Footwear? What a Croc!   *111*

Testosterone Always Aims Low   *114*

Bald is Beautiful   *117*

If I'd Known I Was Going to Live This Long . . .   *120*

REBOOT

Hello Central, Get Me Nostalgia   *125*

No Spam, Thank You, Ma'am   *128*

If the Shoe Fits, Shuck It   *131*

Me and Mustang Sally   *134*

Potholes are Good for Us   *137*

A Cyberfridge? Thanks But No Thanks   *140*

Slow Down, You Move Too Fast   *143*

Seemed Like a Good Idea at the Time   *146*

Got a Problem? Use Your Head   *149*

Snoozing is Good for You   *152*

Measure for Measure   *155*

Keep It Simple, Sony   *158*

All the News That's Fit to Click   *161*

We're Next!   *164*

Time on Our Hands   *167*

THE SHALLOW END OF THE GENE POOL

Kids Will Be Kids—If We Let Them   *173*

And for My Next Trick . . .   *176*

On Island Time   *179*

Feud for Thought   *182*

You Say Soy Latte, I Say Double-Double   *185*

What's the Problem, Officer?   *188*

Mr. Peanut for Premier!   *191*

We Have Met the Enemy . . .   *194*

Life Can Be a Ditch   *197*

A Flagon of the Grape 200
Ouch! That Hurts! 203
Putting the Fan in Fanatic 206
Goodbye Nursing Home, Hello Room Service 209
Earth to Arthur Btfsplk: Stay Home! 212

LAME AS A DUCK

Good News is No News 217
The Sound of Silence 220
It Was a Dark and Stormy Night 223
Dead Ants are My Friends 226
The Duh Vinci Code 229
Hear Ye, Hear Ye! 232
Welcome to Blogworld 235
Two Pennys for Your Thoughts 238
The Art of the Headline 241
Virgin Ears for Vintage Music 244
Book Tours: a Fate Worse than Death? 247
Evolution? Watch Your Mouth 250
Extra! Extra! Read All About It! 253
The Wonderful World of Words 256

VENUSIAN LIZARD KINGS

Paranoid? Who's Paranoid? 261
Fads That Don't Fade 264
Nudes and Prudes 267
If It Itches, Don't Wear It 270
But Is It Art? 273
Enough to Drive You to Drink 276
Mr. Fix-It I Ain't 279
Sign Here, Please 282
Advertising That's *Really* in Your Face 285
Bionic Manhood? No Thanks 288
Anyone for Finger Food? 291
Hey You! Yeah, I'm Talking to You! 294
Extreme Tourism 297
Wretched Excess 300

ANIMAL,
MINERAL,
VEGETABLE

Those Revolting Animals

One of my favourite poems is by an old white geezer by the name of Walt Whitman. It starts: "I think I could turn and live with animals. They are so placid and self-contain'd . . ."

They also forgive a lot, animals do. We leash them and saddle them; harness and hobble them; tether, corral and kennel them. We also do things to them in scientific research labs that would make a Josef Mengele blush.

And do they revolt? They do not. They wordlessly forgive us. As Whitman says:

> *They do not sweat and whine about their condition,*
> *They do not lie awake in the dark and weep for their*
> *sins . . .*

Animals, alas for them, are beasts of infinite forgiveness.

Well, almost. Fact is, an increasing number of incidents seem to indicate that maybe, just maybe, our longtime beasts of burden are beginning to cotton on to the dirty tricks we two-legged fellow tenants have been playing on them. And maybe, just maybe, they're getting fed up and unwilling to take it any more.

I refer you to the case of Jerry Allen Bradford, a Floridian moron who decided to get rid of a litter of unwanted puppies by shooting them with his .38-calibre pistol. He explained later, "I couldn't find homes for them."

Fortunately, one of the puppies beat Bradford to the draw, brushing the trigger with his paw and putting a slug through Bradford's wrist. The Florida Humane Society found homes for the puppies. The Florida justice system has likewise made room for Bradford. In the county jail.

Animal insurrection. It's everywhere. Ask Australians in Canberra. Cause of their alarm? Rioting 'roos. An unseasonable drought has dried up kangaroo watering holes throughout the surrounding area, forcing the creatures into Canberra's parks and gardens. And the marsupials aren't meek and gentle about it. Adult kangaroos stand as high as a man and can kick like a mule—a mule with a shiv in the form of a sharp central claw attached to each rear paw. A kangaroo's favourite tactic is to hold prey in its front paws and disembowel it with the rear ones. Never get between a thirsty kangaroo and a watering hole.

And that goes double for a drunken moose.

Most Canucks know that moose are shy and elusive animals, seldom seen in the woods, much less in built-up areas. At least that's the way it works when the moose are sober. Once they get into the sauce, moose become monsters.

Ask the Swedes. Sweden has a moose population of some three hundred thousand. Normally these Nordic moose are law-abiding, even timid, but each autumn many of them get into windfalls—wild apples that fall from the trees, ferment on the ground and turn into a form of backwoods hooch. Moose gobble them up, and that's when all hell breaks loose.

Swedish police recently juggled reports of inebriated moose blundering into traffic, crashing into living room windows, staggering into empty swimming pools—even executing home invasions. Kari Lindeman lives in a small town in central Sweden called Karlskoga. One evening, he was watching television with his daughter when a tonne of stewed moose came through the patio door.

That's *through* the patio door. It was closed and locked at the time. The moose skidded across the living room floor, smashed the TV, tore the curtains off their rods, trashed some floor lamps and a chesterfield, then staggered out the shattered patio door again.

"It was terrifying," said Mr. Lindeman. "We don't live in the woods . . . we'd never seen a moose in the neighbourhood before."

Nothing uglier than a mean moose drunk. Unless it's a larcenous beaver.

I refer you to the case of the Lucky Dollar Casino heist in Greensburg, Louisiana, recently. Thieves got away with seventy thousand dollars, but after some superb detective work, Louisiana police managed to track down more than half the loot.

In a beaver dam in the nearby Amite River. Police theorize that the casino bandit panicked and threw the loot into the river, after which the beavers, delighted to encounter a source of free wallpaper, grabbed the bills and used them to line the inside of their dens.

That's the official theory. Me, I think Louisiana authorities have unwittingly uncovered just one underground cell of a sophisticated money laundering scheme designed to finance animal insurrection around the world.

Pistol-packing puppies in Florida? Unruly 'roos in Australia? Unglued ungulates in Sweden? Coincidence? I don't think so. My advice: go give Rover a dog bone right now. Stroke your cat. Make sure Polly has plenty of crackers. We need to mend this rift before things get ugly.

Slippery Jack and the Shameless Stinkhorn

I'll never badmouth autumn rain again. Turns out those September deluges blessed much of British Columbia with an almost unprecedented bumper crop of mushrooms. Who knew? Not me. Aside from being able to tell a portobello from a shiitake in the produce department, I know nothing about mushrooms. Well, correction: I know next to nothing. Because I signed up for a mushroom identification lecture recently. I knew it was going to be interesting when the person at the door shook her head and said, "Man, this mushroom lecture always brings out the weirdos."

Now on Salt Spring that's saying something. She had a point. The room was packed. And more than a little intimidating because unlike me, these were clearly people who knew their 'shrooms. Questions tended to be along the lines of: "Is it possible to find the *Cantharellus infundibuliformis* growing in conjunction with the *Cantharellus cibarius,* and do they fruit serially?"

First thing I learned: I had a lot to learn. There are over two thousand species of mushroom on Vancouver Island alone, and that's not counting the subspecies, mutants and mavericks that seem to be almost as common as the fungi with name tags. But I had a dirty little secret. I wasn't working towards a degree in mycology. I just wanted a few tips for scarfing free food from the forest. I wanted to know how to ID one or two mushroom species that I could eat and that wouldn't kill me.

That is the mushrooms' dirty little secret: some can make you quite ill, others can put you on a Grateful Dead magic carpet ride and a few can shut down your liver or blow out your kidneys. Some are so deadly you don't even have to eat them. Our lecturer told of a group who ate some questionable mushrooms with no ill effects. However, the cook died from inhaling the fumes from the frying pan.

Identification is crucial—and not easy. Mushrooms can look like anything from neon dental floss to a wine glass to a beach umbrella to a gypsy's fan to a brain tumour. Esthetically the shapes range from shockingly erotic to profoundly repulsive. In seeking the edible mushroom, beauty is not a factor.

But you gotta love the names. Slippery jack, shaggy mane, donkey's ear, black brain jelly, blue footed scaly tooth and my overall favourite: the shameless stinkhorn. I'm told you smell that one long before you spot it. Of course they all have their stodgy Latin names—*Agaricus bisporus, Tricholoma lascivum* . . .

But even mycology professors can have a sense of humour. You know those little puffballs? The ones you squeeze and they poot out a blast of spores? Their proper name is *Lycoperdon americanum.* Translates as Yankee wolf fart.

But not all mushrooms are as readily identifiable as the puffball. Even the experts classify many as just LBM or LWM. Little brown mushroom or little white mushroom.

Add the fact that so many mushrooms are could-be-this-could-be-that to the fact that so many come with names like the sickener, deadly gallerina, destroying angel, and death cap . . . and I'm still just a teensy bit leery about skipping off into the woods, Little Red Riding Hood-like, to fill my wicker basket with fungi. I think I'll be a responsible shopper for the rest of this mushroom season and just browse the forest. See if I can differentiate between the common and the false chanterelles; learn to tell my blushing from my death cap amanitas by sight rather than bite.

After all, it's not as if I'm desperate. If I'm suddenly overcome with a mushroom jones, I've got options. Portobello. Or shiitake.

Clearing the Deck

Boy, this is complicated. I don't know whether to start by explaining about my tree house, or my raccoons, or the fact that I smell like a urinal.

Okay not *exactly* like a urinal, more like those deodorant pucks they put in urinals. I smell like a deodorant urinal puck because of the raccoons. In my tree house.

See, I have this tree house. It's a modest loft up in some tall cedars where I like to go and watch the sunset. Or used to. Until the raccoons took it over.

Nothing against raccoons. They're very cute with their little bandit masks and stripy tails, and they don't howl like coyotes or chew electrical wires like squirrels.

But they eat a lot. And after they eat they leave calling cards. All over the deck of my tree house. I wouldn't complain if I was sharing the tree house with one raccoon. Or even a mom and a couple of kids.

But judging from the deposits I find each morning, I'm playing host to a West Coast raccoon convention every night.

Now as a kid I worked at the stockyards, and I've mucked out stalls in a horse barn. Believe me, raccoons can hold their own with horses and cattle. Actually, I guess "hold" is the wrong verb. If raccoons could "hold" anything, we wouldn't be having this conversation.

I know what a farmer would do in this situation, but I'm an old peacenik. Termination with extreme prejudice was out of the question from the get-go.

Dogs? I have two dogs. But they are certified layabouts. They know the Alpo will be in the bowl come sundown regardless of their performance on night patrol. Besides, raccoons are way smarter than dogs.

So what to do? Live trap them? Well, live traps are expensive. And besides, that would catch me one raccoon. I've got about thirty-five. I was looking for a group solution.

I tried wrapping the trunks of the cedars in polyethylene. The coons just dug their claws in deeper and trudged on up to the tree house. I tried a tiny electric perimeter fence. The coons daintily stepped over it.

I bought some expensive pest powder guaranteed to discourage all kinds of rodents. I believe the raccoons ate it.

A biologist friend assured me that the answer was to sprinkle mountain lion urine around the deck.

Yeah. That would be good. If I knew an incontinent mountain lion.

"Try mothballs," somebody else advised. "Raccoons hate the smell of mothballs." All right! I bought a box of mothballs, made up a half-dozen net bags and placed them hither and yon on the tree house deck.

And watched as the mothballs disintegrated in the rain.

I was buffaloed. I remember standing at a urinal in the BC Ferries terminal (I do some of my best thinking there), muttering to myself, "I need something that smells bad but won't dissolve in moisture."

It was my Eureka moment. The solution to my problem was practically at hand. It was staring me right in the face.

Urinal deodorant pucks! If raccoons hate mothballs, they'll *despise* urinal deodorant pucks! And urinal deodorant pucks are used to moisture.

Just to set BC Ferries custodial minds at ease, I want you to know I bought my own. At a janitorial supply store in Victoria. Bought 'em, brought 'em home and dished them out like poker chips all over the deck of my tree house.

Did it work? Too early to say. I'm going to give it a couple of nights, then pop up to the tree house and see what's what.

But I can tell you this, if the smell of those pucks deters raccoons the way it's deterred my friends, neighbours and folks on the bus, I'll be getting my tree house back to myself really soon. All to myself.

Only Connect

All the lonely people. Where do they all come from?
—THE BEATLES

Not just people. Whales too. Away out in the Pacific, just off our west coast, marine biologists have been tracking a baleen whale of some kind—for the past twelve years. No one has seen this whale, but they hear his calls via submarine tracking hydrophones. They know it's the same whale because he "broadcasts" at fifty-two hertz, at a much higher frequency than any known whale species. The scientists say that the whale's voice has deepened over the years, perhaps through aging, but it's still very recognizable.

Think about that for a moment. A solitary creature, big as a freight car, moving through the ocean depths, calling, calling. There are few sounds more haunting, to the human ear at least, than the call of a whale. No one knows whether the mystery whale is a blue, a fin or a humpback, but if it's a blue, it could have a life expectancy of 120 years. Who knows how long it was calling before scientists picked it up. Who knows how many more years it will call before it dies. Or finds the other whale it's searching for.

All the lonely mammals . . .

In Finland recently, a sixty-year-old tax auditor had a heart attack at his desk and died. Nobody noticed for two days.

In Italy, Giorgio Angelozzi—an eighty-year-old widower who

lives outside Rome—got so desperately lonely he placed an ad in a newspaper. The ad said that Angelozzi was willing to pay five hundred euros a month to any family willing to "adopt" him as a grandfather.

I'm happy to report that he was besieged with offers from as far away as New Jersey and New Zealand, and he's settled in with a family near Milan—but isn't it sad that he had to take out a want ad?

Are you that lonely? I've got a solution for you. Just call 510-872-7326 and ask for Marc. Marc Horowitz. I'm serious. He wants to know if you want to go out for a bite to eat sometime.

Honestly.

It all started last September when Marc, a twenty-eight-year-old San Franciscan, was working as an assistant on a photo shoot for a Crate and Barrel housewares catalogue. The set he was decorating contained one of those dry-erase boards people use to scribble reminders to themselves. "That looks too blank," Marc thought to himself. So he took out a Sharpie and scribbled a phone number across the board.

A real phone number, 510-872-7326. It gets you Marc's personal cell phone.

When the ad appeared in the catalogue, some readers glommed on to the fact that the phone number wasn't a fake, and Marc's phone started ringing. The first call was from a curious guy named Jake in Kansas. Marc said, "Why don't I fly out to Kansas and have dinner with you?" And he did.

Then there was a call from a New Hampshire grandmother. And a Florida firefighter. A Massachusetts trucker offered him "a place to crash." A Georgia bookseller promised him "a mean lasagna" if he dropped by. A caller from Maryland left this message: "It's because of you that I have a renewed hope in mankind."

At first Marc thought he would take maybe three months off and visit a few dozen people, but his phone kept ringing. So he traded in his pickup for a minivan, sublet his San Francisco apartment and threw a huge garage sale to raise cash for a journey criss-crossing the continent for at least a year.

Point of the exercise? Well, Marc is a conceptual artist, so he's turned this into a performance art project and possibly a book—but it's way more than that. It's a statement about the way we live. We've wired the planet for communication. We've got cell phones and BlackBerrys, Palm Pilots and computer chat rooms. But for all our internet "connectedness," we don't look each other in the eye very often.

"It's about illuminating the importance of conversation between strangers," Marc says. "We just plug into our computers and think that's the way to live, but old-fashioned face-to-face is what it's all about.

"It's about really listening and knowing that everybody has something to say and that their stories are fascinating. This is real conversation with real people—it's something you can't buy."

510-872-7326. Ask for Marc.

A-Hunting We Won't Go

There is a passion for hunting something deeply implanted in the human breast.

—Charles Dickens

I like to check in with the hunting fraternity from time to time, just to see what's up. I'm not a hunter myself, though I used to be as a kid. I fired everything from slingshots and bows and arrows to a .22-calibre bolt-action rifle and a twelve-gauge shotgun, but I gave it up when I realized that while I loved hunting, the killing part bummed me out. And one day, after watching the light fade from the eyes of a fox I'd shot, I decided I could find more enlightened things to do with my spare time.

But to each his own. I understand the magnetic pull of hunting for some folks. Well, mostly I do. I must admit I'm having some trouble wrapping my mind around the hunting saga that unfolded in British Columbia's Rocky Mountains. One Christopher Ott, a "trophy" hunter from Naples, Florida, planned to take his favourite rifle up a BC mountainside and blast the bejesus out of the biggest Rocky Mountain bighorn ram his certified hunting guide could lead him to. Mr. Ott would be the only hunter on the mountain. That's because the hunting season wouldn't be open yet. But that's okay. It was all perfectly legal. Mr. Ott paid for the privilege of hunting alone and out of season.

He paid US$150,000.

To the BC government.

The abiding irony here is that the provincial government planned to use Ott's hundred and fifty grand to *promote sheep conservation.* Excluding, of course, the ram whose head would be hanging on Mr. Ott's wall.

Oh well. At least the nimrod would be taking the trouble to come all the way to Canada to make his kill. He could have just turned on his computer and bagged his bighorn online. Or a black-buck antelope or a wild boar or just about any other wild animal that's walking around on a ranch just outside San Antonio, Texas. That's where North America's first internet hunting service was offered. For a hefty fee, any hunter (or psychopath, for that matter) with a computer anywhere in the world got to manipulate a camera and to "virtually" aim and fire a gun and kill his chosen animal in real time. For an extra fee, ranch hands would ship the head and meat back to wherever the "hunter" lived.

The idea is so revolting that even some hunters oppose it. Two dozen US states have banned the practice. Texas banned it as well—but initially planned only to ban hunting of animals native to the Lone Star State.

So is that what we need to stop such idiocy—more laws?

Umm, maybe not. There's evidence that the only bigger nutjobs than extreme hunters on the loose are certain lawmakers who seek to control them. Consider the plight of some farmers in England who are plagued with crows and starlings eating their crops.

The British Department of Environment, Food and Rural Affairs has given the problem due deliberation and ruled that the farmers do have the right to shoot the birds, but only if they give the birds a "last-chance" option, by shouting, waving coloured stream-ers or employing other "frightening techniques." Failure to try to scare the birds can result in a $13,000 fine, a six-month stretch in the slammer or both.

It gets even wackier in Australia. A farmer named Glen Steinhardt in Murgon, Queensland, appealed to the state's Environmental Protection Agency to help rid him of his starling problem. He reck-oned that upwards of five thousand birds a day were flying in and destroying his wheat and sorghum crops. The Queensland EPA issued a permit allowing Steinhardt to shoot eighty-seven birds—but only if he spreads the kill over an eighty-five-day period.

Steinhardt shakes his head, pointing out that when trucks passing his farm drive through the swarms of birds, they usually kill "50 or 60 in one strike."

But the EPA has no problem with that. Those are "accidental" killings.

On the bright side, lawmakers have managed to draw a curtain on that piece of preposterous British pageantry that features half-snockered, horse-riding aristocrats dressed like clowns accompanied by baying hounds, chasing a fox to exhaustion, whereupon the animal is ripped apart by the dogs. Yes, friends, the infamous British foxhunt has been officially declared illegal.

"The unspeakable in full pursuit of the uneatable," Oscar Wilde dubbed it.

Imagine what Oscar would have to say about the Newfoundland seal hunt.

You Say Tomato,
I Say Yuck

"Come quickly! I am tasting the stars!"

So spake a venerable Benedictine monk by the name of Pierre Perignon in a French vineyard nearly four centuries ago. He had just put to his lips a brand new variety of wine for the first time. The world would come to know this wine as champagne.

I wonder what the old monk would say if I could guide him down the produce aisle of any modern Canadian supermarket and persuade him to bite into a "vine-ripened" imported tomato.

My guess is he'd say something like, "Mon Dieu—I am tasting cardboard!"

Most of our tomatoes during the winter come from Florida. The Sunshine State ships out about half a billion kilograms annually, and Canada is the number one export market.

My question is, Why? Why do we continue to purchase and eat these tasteless blobs? Exactly what the hell have they done to the good old "love-apples" that used to taste so fine?

Actually, I can answer that question. They've graded them, just like eggs. A number one tomato is firm, smooth-skinned and almost perfectly spherical. A number two tomato is round and only slightly rough. A number three is just a little misshapen and perhaps ever so slightly blemished.

Notice something missing there, kiddies? That's right—taste. There are absolutely no points awarded for what a tomato does to your palate.

That's because taste doesn't even register on the agriculture industry's radar screen. Over the past half-century, plant engineers have busted their humps to breed new tomato varieties that have greater yields, hardier pest resistance and shorter growing seasons.

But Donald Davis of the University of Texas Department of Chemistry and Biochemistry says we paid a price for those "advances."

"When you select for yield," says Davis, "crops grow bigger and faster, but they don't necessarily have the ability to make or uptake nutrients at the same faster rate."

Which means not only does the Brave New World tomato not taste anything like the tomatoes grandma used to grow, it's a pale reflection in the nutrition department as well. A study conducted by the aforementioned University of Texas concluded that a typical tomato grown today contains forty percent less vitamin C, forty percent less protein and forty percent fewer minerals than a tomato grown in 1950.

No wonder they taste so bad.

Solution? Easy. All Florida has to do is start shipping Joe Procacci's tomatoes. Joe is a Florida tomato grower who does produce tomatoes just like grandma used to grow. They're luscious, succulent, aromatic and very, very popular. Just three years after Joe started marketing them to grocery stores, his sales tripled.

Unfortunately, Joe's tomatoes have one other characteristic that separates them from the others: they are ugly. Kinda lumpy and misshapen with irregular bumps and bulges. In fact the official name of the variety he created is the UglyRipe.

And that's the problem. The Orlando-based Florida Tomato Committee, which vets all tomatoes that leave the state, has banned the sale of Joe Procacci's UglyRipes because they're, well, too ugly.

The committee claims it hasn't banned Procacci's produce at all. He just has to throw out the fruits that don't come up to the number two grade—you know—smooth-skinned, firm and almost perfectly round.

Which is to say, pretty well every UglyRipe tomato Procacci grows. Recently, come harvest time, he ended up ploughing under about forty tonnes of tomatoes—*every day.*

That's why this winter you will search in vain at your supermarket for Procacci's homely provender. The UglyRipe is not available. That is why the tomatoes you buy will uphold the tradition of winter store-bought tomatoes in Canada. They will slice well, fry nicely, stew adequately, keep indefinitely.

And taste like mulched Yellow Pages.

Nice and round, though.

The Dog Days of Winter

Funny how dogs manage to leave their paw prints on my life, no matter where I happen to be. One day I'm sitting under a thatched *palapa* hut on a beach in Mexico, trying to coax a *perro* named Lobo to share my quesadilla. (What's the Spanish for "Here, boy!"?) And one week later I'm spread-eagled out like a flapping foxtail on a car aerial, clutching the back of a dogsled and trying to remember the Inuit phrase for "Stop, dammit!"

That's the thing about sled dogs—no problem getting them to "mush." In fact, that may be the *only* word they respond to. All they want to do is run. I found that out recently by spending a day at the Timberwolf Resort about a half an hour out of Sault Ste. Marie, Ontario. They keep eighty-nine (yes, eighty-nine) sled dogs at the resort, and for a modest fee you can pick out four of them to take you for a, well, wilderness adventure.

Actually it's not quite that simple. One of the resort pros will select your dogs for you (it's a question of intercanine chemistry), but it's a hands-on experience after that. You get to pick your sled and then you get to hitch your own dogs to it.

Is it scary, hauling semiwild dogs around with your bare hands? Not at all. These dogs don't growl or bite. In fact they barely seem to notice humans. They have their little doggie brains fixed on one goal only: to run flat out, full tilt, pedal-to-the-metal until they can't run any more.

Besides—and I've put off mentioning this because I didn't want to spoil that intrepid Sergeant-Preston-of-the-Yukon image I've been building—the fact is, modern-day sled dogs are kinda . . . puny.

Really. They're not like the massive, barrel-chested, Schwarzenegger-shouldered sled dogs of days gone by. Those dogs—huskies and malamutes mostly—are box-office massive and powerful. They could haul a grand piano up the CN Tower, but their ugly little secret is that all those muscles slow them down. They don't have a lot of endurance. Modern-day sled dogs are a crossbreed of husky and hound, resulting in a mutt that looks like the canine equivalent of the ninety-eight-pound weakling in the old Charles Atlas ads. They're scrawny and nondescript, tipping the scales at maybe fourteen, sixteen kilograms.

But they can run all day.

Interesting things happen when you crossbreed dogs. Ever heard of a Labradoodle? That's what you get when you cross a poodle with a Labrador retriever. The result is an intelligent, gentle dog with great allergy resistance and (Martha Stewart would be pleased) no shedding problem. The Labradoodle is not yet an officially recognized breed, but that hasn't stopped people from lining up to buy the dogs.

Some other poodle-gene-pooling experiments that seem to be panning out involve Yorkshire terriers and schnauzers. The result: Yorkipoos and Schnoodles.

Mind you, it doesn't always work out. Experts say crossing a Newfoundland with a St. Bernard would give you a disease-prone hybrid with hips like Silly Putty. And mating a pug with a Pekinese has produced pups with a distressing propensity for having their eyeballs pop right out of their sockets.

And what would crossing a pit bull with a Doberman produce? I dunno, maybe a Great White Shark?

Actually I've got no problem with pit bulls—it's the people who choose them who need a saliva test. Sure, some pit bulls are gentle and kind and vote only NDP. Same goes, no doubt, for some salt-water crocodiles. The fact remains that if a pit bull does go postal on you, he's got the teeth and jaws to crush your bones to porridge. I well remember the advice I got from a cop I interviewed on the subject of pit bulls years ago. When I asked him how I should defend myself against an attacking pit bull, he deadpanned, "Offer him your least useful arm."

Actually there is a place for pit bulls in this world, and that place is New York City. Gotham's Animal Care and Control Department (we used to call it the Dog Pound) has announced that it is officially renaming pit bulls. Henceforth they shall be known as "New Yorkies." Director Ed Boks says the name change is appropriate because pit bulls and native New Yorkers are both unfairly viewed as surly and belligerent. In fact, says Boks, "New Yorkers are some of the most generous and open-hearted people I've ever met."

Yeah, right, Ed.

New Yorkers and pit bulls: a crossbreed made in heaven.

How Does Your Garden Grow?

The more one gardens, the more one learns. The more
one learns the more one realizes how little one knows.
—Vita Sackville-West

Ah, autumn. Bitter-sweet, happy-sad autumn. From my window I can see the big-leaf maples shimmying into their annual striptease; overhead, disciplined chevrons of geese practise aerial manoeuvres preparatory to blowing this pop stand. It's autumn all right. And once again I have been defeated.

No. "Defeated" is too kind. I have been routed. Shamed. Humiliated. Cruelly slam-dunked and left for dead. I refer, of course, to my garden.

Well, not garden exactly. I refer to that misbegotten patch of rogue real estate in my yard that was by now supposed to be a splendid cornucopia of succulent vegetables and sensual fruits hanging heavy on the vine and fair bursting out of their skins.

It is to whimper brokenly. My sweet corn looks impressive from a distance. The stalks stand well over head high, green and robust. But the ears they support are a cruel misshapen joke. More like nubbly baby fingers, pale white and juiceless. And tomatoes? Hah. If memory serves (and it will have to), I planted four varieties: a beefsteak, a Roma, one red and one yellow cherry tomato plant. I stand to harvest, if I can be bothered, a pants-pocket's worth of bright green marbles, hard as jade and just as juicy.

Well, I lie. My tomatoes aren't all green. Two of them turned brown. Before they died.

My summer's labour has produced a sadistic parody of a garden. Cabbages the size of snooker balls. Peas that look like mummified apostrophes. Carrots worthy of a backyard plot in Chernobyl.

Old Edgar up the street looks over my Edenic ground zero and nods sagely. "Oh ya. Cold spring. Way too much rain in April and May. Ground never really warmed up in time."

Old Edgar is too kind. Neither grey skies, excess moisture nor clammy, unresponsive earth caused my horticultural calamity. It was me and my Black Thumb.

This year's it-is-to-laugh "crop" is but the latest variation on a traditional theme that unspools every fall as cyclically and predictably as the seasons themselves. I plant a garden, nurture it faithfully, then stand by with my Lee Valley hoe in hand and watch it sicken and die. Not only am I a rotten gardener, I'm a slow learner.

My garden is seldom this bad, but it's never up to much. I remember one autumn when I managed to glean a few goodies from the earth. Emboldened by semi-success I was foolish enough to do a cost-benefit analysis of my harvest. Just how much money was I saving by eating home-grown instead of store-bought? I toted up the price of seeds, fertilizer, tomato cages. Not to mention the unexpected: polypropylene netting to discourage rabbits, Back-Eze tablets for my overwrought lumbar region and twenty bucks' worth of vintage clothing from Value Village to dress my scarecrow.

Even discounting my own blood, sweat and tears at minimum wage, I calculated that the garden tomatoes that graced my dinner table set me back about $29.95 apiece.

Discouraged? Hell no. (Did I mention that I was a slow learner?)

I have a brand new plan for next year's garden. It's all based on some nutritional research I came across in an obscure agricultural journal. Listen to this:

Protein content of broccoli: 3.0 mg. Of lamb's quarters: 4.2 mg.

Calcium content of leaf lettuce: 18 mg. Of purslane: 65 mg.
Magnesium content of leaf spinach: 49 mg. Of dock: 63 mg.

For you nongardeners out there, let me explain what lamb's quarters, purslane and dock are.

Weeds! Common, garden and nongarden variety junk plants. Stuff that I've blistered my palms and cricked my back to hack out of my garden for years. Turns out they're more nutritious than the produce I've (not) been growing.

I can harvest these things, folks. Hell, they're in my garden, prime for harvesting right now. Along with amaranth (three times the iron of lettuce) and dandelion (twice the calcium of spinach).

"A weed is no more than a flower in disguise." James Russell Lowell said that.

"I'm going to have a great garden next year." I said that.

Did I mention that I am a slow learner?

Cow Tipping:
the Udder Truth

There have been some classic urban legends in my time—the choking Doberman, the cement-filled Cadillac, the exploding toilet, the charbroiled scuba diver found in the ashes of a forest fire—but none have been quite as hardy or long-lived as the Cow Tipping urban legend.

More of a rural legend, actually, but as robust a yarn as any city slicker ever dreamed up. Urban—and rural—legends all share three characteristics. Number one: they stretch the bounds of credulity completely out of shape. Number two: they are spectacularly funny, horrific or both. Number three: the teller of the legend always vouches for its veracity, but second hand. It happened to his cousin or her landlord or the best friend of a good buddy down at the plant.

Oh, and one other thing they share: urban or rural legends are invariably bogus. Never happened anywhere, anytime. This, despite the eagerness of believers to swear on a stack of *People* magazines that the stories are absolutely one hundred percent swear-to-God true.

So it has always been with cow tipping. I first got wind of the alleged practice many years ago while having a beer with a couple of alumni from the Ontario Agricultural College in Guelph, Ontario. They assured me that certain college colleagues of theirs (not themselves, you notice) occasionally got tanked up at a tavern, then drove out in the country looking for a little action.

When they spied a herd of unsuspecting Holsteins, they would get out of the car, crawl over the fence, tiptoe up to the nearest sleeping bovine, gather on one side of her, deftly flip the beast over and run triumphantly back to the car.

There are a number of unlikely aspects to this story. For one thing, Messrs. Molson and Labatt could not supply enough beer to invest flipping a cow on its side with any significant entertainment value. Moreover, it would be damn hard to even *locate* a herd of cows deep in the country in the middle of the night. Unless you used flashlights, in which case you could expect a reception featuring barking farm dogs, stampeding cattle and irate farmers toting twelve-gauges loaded with rock salt.

And then there are the cows. Contrary to popular belief, cows do not sleep standing up. They doze, but they don't sleep. Also contrary to popular belief, cows are not always docile, placid followers of Gandhi. I used to work in the Ontario Public Stockyards, and I still have scars on my legs where various Holsteins and Herefords registered their displeasure with swift and vicious kicks.

And oh yeah, cows are also heavy. A decent-sized Holstein can easily tip the scales over the two-tonne mark. Imagine yourself and a couple of drunken buddies going up to a full-size Buick and flipping it on its side.

Got that? Now imagine it as a cowhide-covered, cranky, full-size Buick with four sharp hooves and a pair of horns.

The pointy kind, not the honky kind.

But don't take my word for it. Check out the work of Margo Lillie, doctor of zoology at the University of British Columbia. She and student Tracy Boechler actually produced a laboratory recreation of a hypothetical cow tip. They concluded that, theoretically, a cow 1.45 metres tall, pushed at an angle of 23.4 degrees relative to ground level, would require 2,910 Newtons of force in order to be displaced from the vertical to the horizontal.

Translated into English, it would take five trained athletes in peak physical condition to tip a cow under ideal conditions—for example, having said cow consume a bushel of Quaaludes washed down by a couple of two-fours to render Bossie sufficiently catatonic not to realize or react to what was happening to her.

"I have personally heard of people trying but failing," notes Ms. Boechler, "because they are either using too few people or being too loud."

"Most of these 'athletes,'" adds Ms. Boechler unnecessarily, "are intoxicated."

So. Reality check time. Cow tipping: fact or fiction? Could a gaggle of giggling, tanked-up frat boys flip a cow on its side?

Sure it's possible. Absolutely.

When pigs fly.

Fritz the Cinema Cat

Many years ago there used to be a TV show called *The Naked City*. It was about New York, and each installment was introduced by a stentorian voice that said the same thing every show: "There are eight million stories in the naked city. This is one of them."

Well, my island doesn't have eight million residents but it does have several thousand, each with his or her own story, and here comes one of them.

I sing of Fritz, well known throughout the length and breadth of Salt Spring. A consummate gentleman of mysterious origin. No one knows exactly where Fritz came from seven years ago, but everybody knows where to find him today. Camped out on the front porch of Central Hall, a.k.a. the Salt Spring Island Movie House. That's where Fritz eats, sleeps, and in his splendid white coat with black highlights, receives visitors. Fritz is the Cinema Cat.

Used to be you'd find yourself in the movie house watching Sean Penn or Liv Ullman up on the big screen, only to feel a presence brushing your legs or a wet nose nudging your hand. That would be Fritz saying hello. Actually that would be Fritz mooching popcorn. When he began to take on the appearance of a fur-covered Orson

Welles, Fritz was banished from the cinema proper, at least during performances, and put on a healthier diet by Cathie Newman, a local SPCA volunteer who also adopted Fritz. She feeds him, grooms him, arranges his necessary shots and got him (sob) neutered.

Fritz took it all well. You could see him most evenings, poised regally outside his personal and quite lavish cat house on the movie house porch, nodding goodnight to departing movie-goers. Fritz was a local character, an island institution. And then one summer day, Fritz was gone. Disappeared.

And shortly after, this email showed up on computers from one end of the island to the other:

> *Urgent alert. As you may know, there is a resident cat at Central Hall named Fritz who has lived at the hall quite comfortably for years with the support of community members along with the SPCA. This afternoon a visitor from Tsawwassen took it upon herself to take Fritz back to the Mainland.*

Well. Once the Salt Spring gumboot telegraph chattered into action, the lady didn't stand a chance. In nanoseconds the entire island, including the SPCA, the RCMP and BC Ferries knew that the absconder was a grey-haired woman in her sixties, driving a red late-model compact car. We further knew that she had been seen buying a cat carrier at the local hardware store and later loading Fritz into the case, putting him in her car and driving away.

The Mounties showed up at the cinema five minutes after the email went out and put out an APB. Concerned locals rushed to Salt Spring's three ferry terminals to eyeball every car leaving the island. BC Ferries workers peered into the back seats of each vehicle that was remotely red, late-model or compact.

No grey-haired lady. No Fritz. Ergo, cat and catnapper were still on the island. What to do? Elementary, my dear Watson—check the B & Bs. The lady was found, and Fritz was rescued and returned to his house on the porch of Central Hall.

Turned out the lady who took him actually meant well. She was concerned that Fritz was living in a dangerous environment with cars whipping in and out of the parking lot. She just wanted to take him to a safer place. But anybody who knows Fritz doesn't agree. "It seems to me that if he's been living there seven years," opined RCMP Constable Lindsay Ellis, "he's quite traffic wise. He's well cared for and well loved. I have no concerns."

And Fritz? Well, Fritz may be the only Canadian that actually looks forward to election days. Because on election day, Central Hall, a.k.a. the Salt Spring Cinema, becomes a polling station.

"He loves Voting Day," says Cathie Newman, his mom. "Fritz loves it because there are so many people around the hall."

And it's not as if Fritz is a good-time Charlie, a freeloader. Not long ago, this notice appeared in our island newspaper's "Rants and Roses" column:

> *Fritz the Cinema Cat would like to give a spray of wild roses to everyone who donated funds for his care in memory of Jim Stuart. Jim, a cat lover, was buried in the cemetery behind Fritz's home recently. Fritz promises to keep the area mouse-free.*

Only on Salt Spring, eh?

CHAOS THEORY

Live More, Work Less

Picture this: you're hustling through the downtown core on your way to the office and already running behind. You wheel around a corner, cell phone in one hand, Starbucks in the other and behold . . . an army of rodents coming at you.

Except they're huge, these rodents. And walking on their hind legs. You can see they're humans wearing rat masks and carrying attaché cases, and each one has a long rat tail poking out of the nether reaches of its business suit. As they scuttle along, they engage in various rattish activities—zigzagging through mazes, chasing after cheese wedges, jumping through hoops.

It's a theatrical enactment of the rat race that too many of us mistake for a viable way of life. This particular bit of street theatre coursed through the streets of downtown Vancouver. It may soon be coming to an urban rat maze near you.

The rat race is a brainwave from a brand new Canadian political . . . well, "force" might be a little strong—a political "faction" calling itself The Work Less Party. The party's mission: to get Canadians off the insane work-till-you-drop-spend-till-you're-broke treadmill that's driving us all mental.

Is this a serious political movement? Could be. The Work Less

Party claims to have three hundred signed-up members and it's officially registered with Elections BC.

Mind you, it's hardly a conventional movement. The Work Less Party is deliberately leaderless and marches—okay, strolls—to a less than galvanizing slogan, "Workers of the world, relax."

Call me perverse, but I like it.

And so, I would imagine, would Matt Watkins. Mr. Watkins is—or was—a twenty-five-year-old professional jewellery maker earning a decent living in Halifax when he suddenly looked around at the orders piled up on one side of his desk and the bills piled up on the other and came to the epiphanic conclusion: This is stupid.

He flipped off his jeweller's loupe, locked the office door, closed his bank account, gave away all his money, his computer, all his home furnishings and most of everything else he owned. Then he embarked on what he called A Year of Buying Nothing.

How's he doing? Well, six months into his mission he hadn't starved or gone to jail. He house-sat a rural home near Halifax for a friend who went south for the winter. He also ate for free and very well—partly through the generosity of friends, but mostly on victuals salvaged from dumpsters outside grocery stores.

"Inside each of those dumpsters is, like, a huge salad," said Watkins. "The stores dump tons of food each week."

There's nothing wrong with most of that food, maintained Watkins. It's merely past its excessively cautious expiry date. Dumpster diving is not a lifestyle most of us would have the nerve to emulate, but Watkins found other ways to stay off the consumer treadmill. He was happy to chop wood to pay for his supper. He would shovel a driveway in return for a place to bunk for the night.

Watkins followed a compass heading directly the opposite of the rest of society. Most of us spend our waking hours chasing a buck. Watkins strolled determinedly in the other direction.

"Money pervades every part of our lifestyle," he said. "We think of our time as money. And we only value people according to how much they contribute to the economy. What I'm trying to do is have meaningful exchanges with people that are mutually beneficial and are not based simply on monetary value."

Revolutionary words for these times. Though I'm sure Thoreau would nod in agreement. Not to mention a few other historical chaps answering to names as various as Buddha, Mohammed and J. Christ.

Something to think about. I also think I'll hold back ten bucks from my Visa payment this month.

That way, if I run into Matt Watkins, I can buy him lunch.

The Camera Doesn't Lie . . . Sometimes

We can now manipulate images to such an extraordinary degree that there is no lie that you cannot tell.

—Sir David Attenborough

There's a hoary old cliché that tells us a picture is worth a thousand words. I'd put the exchange rate at more like a billion words. For some pictures anyway.

I'm thinking of the photograph of George W. Bush grinning cockily on the deck of a US Navy aircraft carrier, resplendent in a macho, form-fitting jet pilot's flight suit, posed under a banner that reads "Mission Accomplished."

There was an image. It led prime time television newscasts from Florida to Frobisher Bay and ran on the front pages of newspapers and magazines around the world.

There were just a few small problems with the story the picture told. The mission (the war in the Middle East) wasn't even close to "accomplished" and the "pilot" was an impostor. The President of the United States did not possess the expertise to taxi a modern jet fighter out of a hangar, much less get it up in the air. And yet the photo worked like a press agent's wet dream. The world bought into it.

Bush—there's no denying it—looked good in the uniform he didn't deserve to wear. Proof of the photo's power showed up in a poll of active-duty members of the US military released just before the last election that Bush won so handily. The poll revealed that sixty-nine percent of soldiers polled trusted Bush as commander-in-chief. Only twenty-four percent could muster any enthusiasm for John Kerry.

The irony drips. John Kerry was a genuine war hero, thrice decorated and wounded in action. Bush not only ducked service in Vietnam, he failed to show up for duty with the Air National Guard in Texas. And yet one carefully staged photo op was so powerful it fooled even military personnel who should have known better.

Photographic images are undeniably powerful, but they can be treacherous as well. Remember George Dukakis? He was putting up a decent run for the White House back in 1988, until he made the mistake of letting himself be photographed popping out of the hatch of an army tank. He was wearing a tank helmet with the earflaps askew and he looked like Snoopy perched on his ersatz Sopwith Camel. Americans started to laugh and they didn't stop until Bush the Elder was elected in a landslide.

Politicians on this side of the border know, too, that a political campaign can turn on the strength of a glossy photo or two. We could ask Robert Stanfield, if he was still around. In 1974 Stanfield was campaigning against Pierre Trudeau for the prime minister's office. His plane touched down at North Bay, Ontario, and Stanfield felt the urge to stretch. He started a game of catch football with some of his entourage. A Canadian Press photographer squeezed off thirty-six shots of the impromptu exercise showing Stanfield catching and throwing the football with practised ease.

For the most part. Stanfield did fumble once or twice—as anyone might. The photographer shipped the raw film off to Toronto for processing. Later, he got a call saying one of his photos would be running on the front page of the *Globe and Mail* the next day. The photographer told Stanfield, "You owe me a beer. I got you on the front page of the *Globe.*"

But it didn't work out that way. The editors in Toronto ignored all the photos that made Stanfield look good and chose a fumble shot. An excruciatingly *bad* fumble shot. Stanfield's horn-rimmed glasses were askew, and he had a grimace on his face that looked like he'd been kicked in the gonads. His knees were knocked together and his bony fingers clutched ineffectively at the ball squirting out of his grasp. Stanfield looked like Ichabod Crane. Another scribe on the tour took one look at the front page and said, "Trudeau just won the election."

And he was right.

Maybe it was the photo that did Stanfield in. Or perhaps it's just that Canadians don't buy into phony heroism as readily as Americans. Stockwell Day's political career began going south the day he decided, as leader of the Canadian Alliance, to dazzle a press conference by swooshing up on a Jet Ski, dressed in a skin-tight wetsuit.

Sort of an aquanaut version of Dubya on the aircraft carrier.

Except it didn't work. The press howled until they cried, and the Canadian general public followed their lead. Day didn't look like a superhero. He looked like a doofus.

Too often a slick photographer can sell us a bill of goods. But sometimes, praise be, the camera doesn't lie.

The Law is an Ass

The worse the society, the more law there will be. In Hell there will be nothing but law, and due process will be meticulously observed.

I'm not exactly sure which disgruntled lawyer-to-be scrawled those words on a marble bathroom wall in the innards of Osgoode Hall in Toronto more than half a century ago, but I think I know what he was driving at. The law, as Dickens warned us, is an ass. An idiot. Three recent cases of jurisprudence gone nuts (all mercifully from south of the border) illustrate the point.

Case number one: Meet Daniel Provencio, aged twenty-eight, a two-time loser incarcerated in a California prison, who is about to take a called third strike. Unwisely he decides to participate in a prison uprising and is promptly shot in the head by a guard firing foam bullets. Daniel Provencio is swiftly taken to the prison hospital and, in accordance with routine penitentiary procedure, securely handcuffed to his hospital bed. He is also assigned an armed prison guard who is instructed to stand by Provencio's bed around the clock.

The only factor that makes this entire procedure slightly Kafkaesque is the fact that a prison doctor has already declared Mr. Provencio clinically brain dead. Aha. But he is still, dead or alive, an inmate. Therefore, according to prison rules, he must be shackled to the bed and guarded by certified prison officials twenty-four hours a day. Why the armed guard nursemaid for a man who can't move a muscle? "Potentially, someone could come in and wheel him out," a prison spokesman explained.

Er, okay, but why the handcuffs? "If we were to unshackle him, we'd have to consult with the prison guards' union."

Cost of the around-the-clock guard: a thousand dollars a day. Ironically Mr. Provencio resolved the dilemma by dying outright after two and a half weeks in the hospital, leaving behind just a little over $160,000 in unpaid medical bills.

Case number two: Meet Daryl Atkins, twenty-seven, of Yorktown, Virginia, a convicted murderer who turned out to be a little too smart for his own good.

This was no mean feat, when you consider that Atkins had officially been declared mentally retarded. In fact it was his designation of mental retardation that saved him from the electric chair. The state of Virginia has a law making it unconstitutional to execute any criminals whose IQs register below seventy. Daryl was home-free with an IQ reading of fifty-nine.

At least he was until he started a long and complicated series of appeals against his conviction. On a hunch the state's legal experts had Atkins take the IQ test over again. He scored seventy-four.

A Virginia psychologist speculates that the jump in Atkins' IQ could be attributable to the "mental stimulation" resulting from frequent talks with his team of lawyers.

Sometime in the spring of this year, a jury will sombrely convene to decide whether Daryl Atkins has become intelligent enough to be worthy of execution by the state of Virginia.

Not bizarre enough for you? Then consider case number three: John Taylor is an inmate at Utah State Prison.

Imagine you are standing with John Taylor in the exercise yard on a blustery January evening in 1998. It is bitterly cold, and Taylor is hunched against the wind, desperately trying to light a Marlboro cigarette. He is handcuffed and surrounded by two prison guards who wait impatiently, stamping their feet against the cold, as Taylor gets his cigarette lit and smokes it hungrily down to the filter.

When Taylor is finished, he grinds out the butt with his heel, turns and re-enters the Utah State Prison.

Where he is escorted to the execution shed, stood against a wall of sandbags and shot to death by a firing squad.

Capital punishment in Utah is still in effect.

But smoking in public buildings? That's a no-no.

Nice Work If You Can Get It

Frankly, I have no taste for either poverty or honest
labor, so writing is the only recourse left for me.
— Hunter S. Thompson

I know whereof the maestro of Gonzo journalism speaks. I have
had many blessings in my life, but one of the greatest is this. Right
here. Writing stuff for you to read.

I am a professional word cobbler. A thought weaver. A mason of
sentences and paragraphs. I look at the world around me, then I sit
down and write about it. That's my job, and I love it.

Which puts me in a rarefied category of working stiffs.
According to a survey conducted by an online job search company
called Workopolis, thirty-two percent of us barely tolerate our jobs.
We consider them just a means of paying the mortgage and putting
food on the table.

For others, it's even worse—seventeen percent of the people
who went to work this morning would just as soon be going to the
dentist.

Think of it: nearly one out of five people loathe and despise what
they do for a living.

Part of the problem is the nature of some jobs. Two-thirds
of the people surveyed said their places of work offered them no

opportunity for advancement. Another thirty percent said their jobs were routine, with no exposure to new experiences.

For those of you who find yourself in the can't-stand-my-job category, I offer one small consolation. It could be worse. There are some really, really lousy jobs out there that probably make yours look like a stroll on the boardwalk. Each year, the magazine *Popular Science* publishes a "Ten Worst Jobs in Science" list. Recently the list included students who, for a measly fifteen dollars an hour, signed an agreement to have pesticide sprayed in their eyes in a University of California study.

Then there were the guys who worked for the US Geological Survey in a remote area of California. Their job was monitoring extremophile microbes. All you need to know about extremophiles is that they are supernaturally stinky and they live in foul-smelling environments. One employee said it was like being surrounded by a hundred "extremely flatulent people."

My worst job? Tar and gravel roofing. Slinging hot pitch around in the blazing sun in the company of a squad of crazed workaholic French Canadians who started at dawn and slaved until they dropped.

But that's nothing compared to a job I witnessed in the Kananaskis Valley of Alberta. I was doing a story on a crew of biologists whose job it was to tag and collar mountain lions. They used a pack of hounds to track and tree the lions. They darted them, fitted them out with radio-transmitter collars and set them free again. Most of the guys in the crew clearly enjoyed their work—except for one, who never seemed to smile.

I found out why. When the crew had a cougar treed and tagged with a tranquilizer dart, Gloomy Gus moved into action. The cougar was on a branch only about six metres over our heads.

As the cougar began to get groggy, Gus slipped a noose attached to a pole around its head and shoulders. The idea was to break the animal's fall and ease it carefully down to the ground.

It meant that Gus had to stand directly under the cougar. He was looking more and more disconsolate.

"How do you know when it's about to lose consciousness?" I

whispered to the other crew members. They grinned like Cheshire cats.

I soon found out. A sure-fire sign that a tranquillized cougar is about to pass out and fall is the loss of bladder control.

All over Gloomy Gus. I wonder if he included that on his work resumé?

Ah, but then there's Tim Byrne. Tim's a Brit who lives in London. According to a story in the *London Sun,* Tim just can't get enough of his job. Even when he goes on vacation to places like Tenerife and Mallorca, Tim looks up folks in his line of work, then pitches in and gives them a hand. For free.

His line of work? Garbage collector. For the past eleven years, Tim has cheerfully hauled trash and hefted garbage cans while his mates were getting sunburned at the beach.

"Rubbish plays such a large role in my life that I simply don't need to get away from it," says Tim.

I suppose that's all it really takes to handle a bad job. A good attitude.

Then again, Tim Byrne never had to stand under an incontinent mountain lion.

Liberal: Just a Four-Letter Word

"When I use a word," Humpty Dumpty said, in rather a scornful tone, "it means just what I choose it to mean—neither more nor less."

"The question is," said Alice, "whether you can make words mean so many different things."

"The question is," said Humpty Dumpty, "which is to be master—that's all."

—LEWIS CARROLL

I have seen more than a few words and phrases get torqued into new and twisted meanings in my day. I remember when Roy Rogers was a cowboy, not a restaurant. I remember when Tim Horton was a hockey player, not a doughnut shop.

I remember when "gay blade" referred to a fun-loving man about town. What's a gay blade today—a bisexual left-winger with the Anaheim Ducks?

And speaking of left-wingers, what have we done to the word "liberal"?

When I was growing up "liberal" was personified—in the political sphere at least—by Lester B. Pearson, a genial, bumptious butterball of a man with an engaging stutter who worked like a beaver and Got Things Done.

Pearsonian liberalism morphed into Trudeaumania, which was stylish, saucy and infinitely more hip.

Then we had the John Turner flyby followed by eight centuries of Jean incoherent-in-both-official-languages Chrétien.

And then we got Paul Martin. When I think of Paul Martin liberalism I think of—I don't know—room temperature Jell-O? Nothing that came out of his mouth had any weight or substance. He wasn't so much Liberal as Blabberall.

If what the feds did to the word "liberal" wasn't confusing enough, consider what provincial governments have accomplished. Remember Robert Bourassa, one-time head of the Quebec provincial Liberals and staunch personal ally of . . .

. . . Brian Mulroney? A Tory?

And look at British Columbia. The premier of BC is Gordon Campbell. Who is also head of the BC Liberal party.

Gordon Campbell a liberal? My dictionary (Canadian Oxford) defines the word as "given freely, ample, abundant, not strict or rigorous."

Calling Campbell a liberal is like calling Genghis Khan the Laughing Buddha.

But Canadian linguistic depredations are as nothing compared to the mugging the word "liberal" has endured south of the border. In the USA, to be called "liberal" is to be slimed with the sleaziest epithet in the political lexicon. It has replaced "commie rat" and "pinko traitor." It is hurled like boiling oil from Republican ramparts on the heads of anyone or any institution that dares to criticize the machinations of the Oval Office.

How could a whole nation turn its back on a word that signifies "open-minded, not prejudiced"? It's enough to drive a country to drink.

And it has. Come with me now to Rudy's Bar in the Hell's Kitchen section of New York. As befits its surroundings, Rudy's is a hole-in-the-wall kind of joint—sawdust on the floor, a jukebox in the corner—no karaoke here. But every Thursday night, Rudy's transforms into something very rare in that country these days.

A hidey-hole for citizens who feel left out of Bushamerica. Thursday nights, New York members of this endangered species make their way to Rudy's for a club meeting.

The club is called, but of course, Drinking Liberally.

And it's catching on. What started as a haven for New York non-Bushies back in 2003 has mushroomed. First a chapter opened in San Francisco. Then Houston copied, followed by Oakland. When the American electorate gobsmacked international opinion by electing The Village Idiot to a second term, they also sent thousands of disenchanted Americans into the arms of Drinking Liberally. Membership soared. Today there are eighty-six chapters of Drinking Liberally spread over thirty-seven states.

What do attendees at a Drinking Liberally get-together actually do? Cry in their beer, obviously. But they also talk about future political campaigns, listen to left-of-centre candidates and generally network with citizens of the same political persuasion.

As the Bush administration begins to discover the gumbo of corruption and incompetence sticking to its cowboy boots, the future of Drinking Liberally can only be described as rosy (not to be confused with pinkish). More and more Americans are finally taking back their democratic right to tell Washington to go to hell.

Who knows? They might even resuscitate the word "liberal."

Lawsuits to Die For

Come with me now to a public schoolyard in Broward County, Florida. Any schoolyard in the county, really. They're pretty much all the same, which is to say, not like schoolyards you'd see anywhere else. You won't find swings in this school playground. Or slides or monkey bars. In fact, no equipment on which, or with which, a child could get—you know—hurt. Another quaint feature of your typical Broward County schoolyard are the signs plastered everywhere. "No Running," they say.

That's right. Kids are not allowed, by law, to run on school property. It's a bit like telling goldfish that swimming is verboten, but it's the law in Broward County.

There is a reason for this absurdity, and it is a familiar one—lawyers. In the past six years Broward County taxpayers have been forced to shell out more than half a million US dollars to settle claims for 189 playground injuries.

"To say 'no running' on the playground seems crazy," allows school board member Robin Bartleman, "but your feelings change when you're in a closed door meeting with lawyers."

Ah well. Frivolous lawsuits launched by extortionate lawyers are nothing new—and not exclusively the domain of the wacky US south. I well remember a lovely abandoned stone quarry near the town of Elora, Ontario. It had steep granite sides and was filled with sparkling green water—a swimmin' hole to die for. Generations of local kids jumped off the rim of the quarry into the water below.

Until one night in the early eighties, when some knuckle-dragging drunk staggered off the edge and managed to break his back in the fall.

Naturally he found himself an obliging lawyer and sued the township—not his fault that he was drunk and stupid, right?

And just as naturally, he won. A million-dollar settlement that all but bankrupted the township and led to the erection of fences around the quarry and signs everywhere explaining that it could be dangerous to one's health to fall off the side of a quarry.

But that was a quarter of a century ago. We must be getting smarter, no?

No.

Not if Vlado Maljkovich's story is any indication. Mr. Maljkovich is five thousand dollars richer, thanks to his recent lawsuit against Correctional Service Canada.

Not that he'll be blowing that dough at the racetrack any time soon. Mr. Maljkovich's lawsuit was against the Fenbrook Institution, a penitentiary north of Gravenhurst, Ontario.

And Maljkovich is in it. Serving time for having murdered his wife and daughter.

So what was the lawsuit about—humiliation and abuse by guards? Harassment from inmates in the exercise yard? Nope—second-hand smoke. Mr. Maljkovich has been forced to endure the agony of cigarette smoke expelled by fellow inmates. Now a court has affixed a five grand price tag on his suffering—and opened the door for lawsuits from every other non-smoking con in the Canadian jail system.

Give Mr. Maljkovich brownie points for chutzpah, if nothing else. Still, he's strictly a minor leaguer compared to Pavel M., another killer presently doing time in Timisoara Penitentiary in Romania.

Pavel M. has also launched a lawsuit—against God.

He's suing the supreme deity for breach of contract. He claims that his baptism was an implicit and binding agreement in which

God was to "keep him from all harm" in return for "various goods and prayers." Since God allowed Pavel M. to fall in with bad company, drink, steal and stab another Romanian to death, it follows that God is in breach of contract and owes Pavel M. big time. No word yet on whether God is seeking legal representation, but if he is, he'll know who to call.

There's a story about God phoning up Satan one afternoon just to shoot the breeze.

"How's it going down there?" he asks.

"Fantastic!" says Satan. "We got an engineer two months ago, and he's installed air conditioning, flush toilets, escalators, water fountains—there's no telling what this guy will come up with next."

God is furious. "You've got an engineer? That's a mistake! He should be here in heaven. Send him up immediately!"

"No way," says Satan.

"Send him up or I'll sue," says God.

Satan cackles. "Sue? Where are *you* gonna find a lawyer?"

I can hear your groan from here. That's the trouble with corny lawyer jokes. Lawyers don't think they're funny. And nobody else thinks they're jokes.

Counting Our Blessings

Indeed, it has been said that democracy is the worst form of government except all those other forms that have been tried from time to time.

—WINSTON CHURCHILL

Winnie was right, you know. We love to bitch and moan about our political leaders—Jack "Motormouth" Layton, Stephen "Hang 'Em High" Harper, Stéphane "Nerd? Moi?" Dion—but do you see any other world leaders you'd trade them in for?

Gordon Brown? Pass. Russia's lemur-eyed Putin? No thanks. Italy's slap-happy scandal magnet Silvio Berlusconi? Forget it. George "The World Is My Oil Well" Bush? I don't think so.

Ottawa may operate on a narrow spectrum that ranges from timid to hapless, but given the morons and madmen the rest of the world endures, that's not so bad.

T'was ever thus. The pages of history are littered with homicidal megalomaniacs who rose to positions of power and proceeded to ladle out grief and misery by the bucket.

Alexander the Great, Attila, Genghis Khan—all guys you didn't want to get on the wrong side of. Cleopatra, the Borgias, Napoleon. Various British kings and Spanish queens. Not a few Popes and sundry Caesars, including Nero, who murdered his own mother and installed his horse in the Roman Senate.

And there are millions of people still alive who remember when monsters named Mussolini, Stalin and Hitler lurched upon the earth.

Ceausescu. Pol Pot. Saddam Hussein.

The beat goes on. South America has groaned under its Perons and Pinochets. And poor Africa is still raddled with genocidal thugs who rule by terror and grind their own people in the dust.

Look around. We could be living under Muammar al-Gaddafi, the Libyan fruitcake who sponsors terrorists, writes incomprehensible "bestsellers" and once deported Palestinian refugees, telling them to "walk back to Palestine."

Or how about North Korea's Kim Jong-il? A dumpy little creep with permed hair, platform shoes and designer sunglasses who arranges elaborate orgies for himself (of food and women) and orders billboards erected that declare "Our Great Leader Is Always with Us" and "We Are Happy."

And all the while his people starve, sometimes to the point of eating grass.

Yeah, Ottawa's looking pretty good—and I haven't even got to Saparmurat Niyazov.

This is a chap you perhaps never heard of, but the people of Turkmenistan (population five million) knew him only too well. Until his death in December 2006 he was their self-appointed President for Life—no annoying and inconvenient four-year terms for Niyazov—and you could tell he really loved his job by the way he kept issuing decrees. He instituted a national holiday in honour of the muskmelon. He also commanded a university student, who was reading a speech praising him, to get her gold teeth removed and replaced with white ones. "Here is the health minister," Niyazov said, waving at one of his flunkies, "He will give you white teeth."

The guy got weirder. He banned beards and listening to car radios. He declared opera and ballet illegal. He ordered television show hosts not to wear makeup because he said he had difficulty distinguishing heavily made-up males from females.

But that's the little stuff. President Niyazov dreamed much bigger than that. He declared that his citizens would remain adolescents until they were twenty-five. Youth in Turkmenistan officially doesn't end until thirty-seven. Old age kicks in at age eighty-five.

Oh yes, and he also ordered an ice palace to be built so that Turkmenistani children could learn to ski.

Did I mention that Turkmenistan is nine-tenths desert? It is one of the hottest hell holes on the planet where summertime temperatures routinely hit fifty degrees Celsius. It is also dirt-poor and a stranger to the concept of air conditioning.

An ice palace should work out just swell.

So by all means speak out about the idiocies of Ottawa and the poltroons and prevaricators who befoul provincial politics. Write incendiary letters to the editor. Call up the local Open Mouth radio show and vent your spleen 'til you run out of breath.

But every once in a while remind yourself that the very fact that we can rant and rave to our hearts' content places us among a very blessed—and tiny—minority on the planet.

Bonehead Bureaucratic Blunders

I know it's early on, but I'm making a prediction. I predict that this year will yield a bumper crop of bonehead bureaucratic blunders the like of which we haven't seen in decades. I'm talking about spectacular, stupefying, stunned decisions rendered by pencil pushers and bean counters around the world. Hey, it's a slam dunk. Look at the Homer Simpson harvest we've already reaped.

Exhibit A: The secondary school administration responsible for the education district incorporating Spurger, Texas, recently announced the end of its hallowed Homecoming Week Reverse Roles Day. This was the one day in the school year on which students were encouraged—nay, strongly encouraged—to wear clothes of the opposite gender. Girls dress as boys and vice versa. This in Texas?

Wait. It gets better. This year some anonymous parent complained that the practice promoted a "homosexual lifestyle."

And so the school deep-sixed the cross-dressing tradition. And replaced it with a requirement that the students dress for the day in . . . military camouflage.

Hey! I said it was Texas.

Exhibit B: London, England. An employee of the British Broadcasting Corporation exits headquarters through a revolving door in the main lobby. Regrettably, said employee gets lead foot caught in revolving door, mangling toe and cracking toenail. Bureaucratic response? A company-wide three-page memo to each and every member of the eight-hundred-strong head office workforce using stick figure graphics to illustrate how to walk through a revolving door safely.

Not that we in the colonies have any reason to smirk and simper. Consider the bureaucratic meltdown in Prince Edward Island, where the Progressive Conservative government came up with a mind-blowing brainwave calculated to save the Island taxpayers thirty thousand dollars a year.

It was ingenious in its simplicity. The PEI government runs this twenty-four-hour suicide hotline, right? Where desperate people can phone in, just before they slash, overdose or jump off Confederation Bridge, and get expert help to talk them out of taking their own lives. Fine. All well and good. But . . . twenty-four hours? Think of the overtime!

The government boffins decided, why not cut the service back to oh, say, banker's hours—nine to five, and no weekends? Huge savings.

Thus a bipolar person in Summerside might dial up the suicide hotline some dark and dreary night and hear, "Hello. You've reached the PEI suicide hotline. No one is in the office right now, but your call is important to us. Please call back during business hours, nine a.m. to five p.m. Monday to Friday. And . . . have a great day."

I'd love to feel superior to the feckless functionaries in PEI, at the BBC and down in Texas, but that would be ill-advised. I live, after all, on Salt Spring Island where the Egg War rages. When it comes to bureaucratic dunderheadedness, we here on the western edge of the country have no right to feel smug.

The Egg War?

It works like this. Farmers have chickens. Chickens lay eggs. People eat eggs. Farmers take the eggs from under the chickens and sell them to hungry people. Simple, right?

Wrong. You're not allowing for the Vancouver Island Health

Authority that insists on inspecting those eggs somewhere between the hen's bum and the consumer's *huevos rancheros*. Which in Salt Spring's case would be admirable, if the Vancouver Island Health Authority actually did anything besides cluck bureaucratically. It doesn't. Eggs are not inspected on Salt Spring because there are no facilities to inspect them. So the farmers simply sell them.

Here's the problem. It's legal for the farmers to sell eggs at the farm gate, but illegal for them to sell eggs at the farmers' market that takes place each Saturday morning five minutes down the road in Ganges.

Same egg. Just moved down the road. Legal at the farm gate. Illegal at the farmers' market.

Stupid? You bet. But Salt Spring wouldn't be Salt Spring if it didn't come up with a solution.

Meet Harry Warner. Superannuated Salt Spring hippie, computer consultant, musician and . . . chicken farmer. Harry showed up at the market last Saturday with several dozen eggs for sale and a plywood frame labelled "Farm Gate" hanging from his neck.

Salt Spring, one. Bureaucrats, no score.

School Boards:
Thick as Planks

In the first place God made idiots. This was for practice. Then he made school boards.

Mark Twain fired off that observation more than a century and a half ago. Since then, mankind has learned to fly, broken the sound barrier and even lobbed a few astronauts up to the moon and back.

And some school boards have just become stupider.

Case in point: the Annapolis Valley regional school board. A hundred and six drama students from Avon View High School in Windsor, Nova Scotia, were looking forward to a live stage production at the Neptune Theatre in Halifax. Their teacher had arranged for buses and overnight accommodation.

The school board vetoed the plan and cancelled the trip. Why? Officially, because the play in question "wasn't on the province's official reading list." But I have to think it was really because the school board members knew full well that the play in question was dangerous propaganda calculated to warp young minds and foment toxic, antisocial attitudes.

So what was this play, a bunch of Bolsheviks acting out *Das Kapital?* A stage adaptation of *Mein Kampf?*

No, it was a production of *To Kill A Mockingbird,* based on the classic novel written by Harper Lee. It's a story set in a small town in Alabama during the Depression. The story is told from the point of view of a six-year-old tomboy, whose lawyer father defends a black man falsely accused of attacking a white woman.

It is, in short, a story about racial prejudice seen through the eyes of a young child. Something you'd think school boards might see some value in sharing with the students under their care.

Wrong. The Annapolis Valley regional school board issued a statement saying that *To Kill A Mockingbird* "would not pass an Education Department bias evaluation."

Strange. The book won the Pulitzer Prize for Fiction. The film adaptation of *To Kill A Mockingbird* got an Academy Award and a Golden Globe Award for "best film for promoting international understanding." What does the Annapolis Valley regional school board know that the rest of the world doesn't?

Well, as Mr. Twain implies, the people in charge of what our kids learn can be passing weird. I had my own run-in with the Alberta education system recently. They wanted to use one of my commentaries in a provincial text book. The commentary was about cars and the pollution they cause. I speculated in the piece that some day, automobiles might be as obsolete as dinosaurs.

The Alberta editors wanted to remove the dinosaur reference.

"Why?" I asked.

The official response: "To respect the tolerance and under-standing of other religious groups. We need to factor in the religious groups who do not believe in dinosaurs."

Do not believe in dinosaurs? I wrote back suggesting that the text book go ahead without my story, as I was not interested in promot-ing bone-headed ignorance.

If it's any consolation, educational idiocy is not restricted to this side of the Atlantic. Recently the city council of Birmingham, England, decided that perhaps it was all right after all for Birmingham kiddies to recite the nursery rhyme "Baa, Baa, Black Sheep."

There had been some anguish that the rhyme was . . . you know . . . racist. The *black* sheep and all?

Actually it wasn't the city council that came to its senses. It was a black mother of three who stood up in the middle of the city council debate and pointed out that "the rhyme is about black sheep, not people."

By the way, those kids at Avon View High in Nova Scotia finally did get to see *To Kill A Mockingbird*—the film version, not the stage play. Their grade eleven English teacher, John Hudson arranged a screening for them in Windsor, and lawyer Jim White treated them.

One of the students, Kathlyn Smith, said, "I liked the movie. For me, it's not really even about race issues. It's the story of one person's childhood."

Think you could explain that to your school board, Kathlyn?

I'll Sue You in My Dreams

I'll probably get sued for the next four words I write:

Dirk and Enid Spendrake. There. I wrote it. As soon as they see their names in print, Dirk and Enid will be on the blower to their lawyers who'll be typing out writs just as fast as their fingers can fly. The Spendrakes will be on my butt just as surely as the sun will rise tomorrow. Oh yeah—they'll sue me all right.

Why not? They've sued just about everybody else.

Over the past few years the Nanaimo, BC, couple has sued: their neighbours, the local police, the RCMP, the town council, a justice of the peace, a couple of unions, several newspaper employees, one judge and innumerable lawyers.

They've been temporarily muzzled by a BC Supreme Court Justice who has issued an order prohibiting Dirk and Enid from filing any more court actions without his say-so—but that won't last. The Spendrakes will just badger the judge, his barber, his chauffeur, his cat—whatever it takes.

And then they'll come after me.

I don't mind. There are so many frivolous lawsuits clogging our courts that I'll be dead and planted before my name even comes up.

It's even worse in the USA where fifty-two thousand lawsuits, many of them ridiculous, are currently wending their tortuous way through the courts. Such as Patricia Frankhouser's. Patricia, who lives in Jeannette, PA, is suing the Norfolk Southern Railway as a result of being hit by one of their trains. Patricia only sustained a few cuts and a broken finger, but her dignity suffered a massive hemorrhage.

She was walking on the tracks, you see, when the train struck her. Her lawsuit maintains that Norfolk Southern should have posted signs alongside the tracks warning people that trains might come along from time to time.

What did she think—that she was on a realllllllly long staircase? The low handrails should have been a clue.

Don't laugh. If current trends are any indication, Patricia will soon be a rich woman and Norfolk Southern will be posting signs along all its trackage that read, "Warning: Trains May Be on Tracks."

Fear of lawsuits is driving a lot of dopey labelling these days. I've got one of those cardboard thingies that you put on your windshield to keep the sun out. It carries a warning in the bottom left hand corner that says, "Please Remove before Driving."

There's an entire website devoted to wacky warning labels. Like the label that appears on a child's scooter that reads, "Warning: This Product Moves When Used."

Or the label attached to a toilet brush cautioning the purchaser that it is "not to be used for oral hygiene."

It would be funny if it wasn't so sad—and some of it's very sad. Such as the two Colorado teenage girls who now have criminal records and a big fine to pay.

All for baking cookies.

Taylor Ostergaard and Lindsey Jo Zellitte had this idea one night. They didn't want to go to a local dance because they figured there would be drinking and fighting, but they wanted to do *something*. Lindsey said, "Why don't we bake some cookies and take them around to the neighbours?"

So they did. Whipped up a huge batch of chocolate chip and sugar cookies, decorated them with paper hearts, then took them around to several homes in the neighbourhood and left them by the front door on paper plates with the message, "Have a great night."

One of the recipients, Wanita Young, aged forty-nine, filed a lawsuit. She claimed she was "frightened" by the unsolicited cookies on her doorstep.

Sad, eh?

Nope, I'll tell you what's sad. A Colorado judge found the two girls guilty and ordered them to pay the woman nine hundred dollars for "distress."

Nice work, judge. You don't know the Spendrakes, do you?

Of All the Gaul!

The French complain of everything. And always.

No, George W. Bush didn't say that, and neither did Winston Churchill. The author of that remark was a chap who knew *les gens de la République* better than most. His name was Napoleon Bonaparte.

It seems that being a leader of the French is even more exasperating than merely observing them from afar. Somebody else once moaned, "How can anyone govern a nation that has 246 different kinds of cheese?"

His name was Charles de Gaulle.

Well, they are an unpredictable people to be sure. Take Brigitte Bardot. The one-time cinema sexpot was on our TV screens a lot in recent springtimes, pouting and pleading with Canada to end the "sickening and barbaric" seal hunt. Perhaps she has a point, but it's interesting to note that when she's not embracing our cute and cuddly seal pups at photo ops, she's slagging gays, Muslims, immigrants and anybody who doesn't happen to have a job. She calls homosexuals "freaks." She's been charged with inciting racial hatred a half a dozen times. She supports the politician Jean-Marie Le Pen, a French bigot who occupies a spot on the political map somewhere between George Lincoln Rockwell and Adolf Hitler. And she opposes mixed marriages.

Lucky for those seal pups they were born white.

The French are nothing if not contrary. Their politicians bad-mouth American belligerence in the Arab world at the same time as French munitions manufacturers shovel warplanes, rocket grenades, tanks and guns out the back door to any Middle Easterner with a valid credit card. Even as an ally, France has often proved to be a trial. During the dark days of World War II, Britain offered refuge to Charles de Gaulle, leader of the Free French. Was de Gaulle grateful? Hardly.

"France has no friends, only interests," he once said. Also, "When I want to hear what France thinks, I ask myself."

After the war, Churchill is reputed to have remarked, "Of all the crosses I have had to bear during this war, the heaviest has been the Cross of Lorraine." That was de Gaulle's symbol of Free France.

And if he didn't say it, he should have.

On the other hand, the French have given us much. Their contributions to the world of wine, cheese and even bread are second to none. The French language is, incontestably, the most beautiful to the ear. French artistes, from Molière to Matisse to Massenet, have enriched the world's cultural mix beyond measure.

Yes, in balance, we could forgive the French their inconsistencies and irrationalities, but for one flaw, one national blemish that cannot be ignored.

They love Jerry Lewis.

Idolize him! In 1984 they made Lewis a commander in the Order of Arts and Letters, France's highest cultural award. Two months later they awarded him the *Legion d'Honneur.* That's the highest honour France can bestow on anybody.

The French besotment with one of Hollywood's goofiest progeny is no one-night stand. As far back as 1965 they were saluting his "comic cinematic genius." In fact, that's the year that French critics chose *The Nutty Professor* as the best film of the year.

Have you *seen* that film? If not, don't. Trust me.

The love affair rages on. Recently the French Ministry of Culture held a special ceremony to elevate Lewis into an even more exalted niche in the French pantheon of fame. They gave him the honorary title of Legion Commander.

Lewis attended the ceremony and, in his quintessentially classy way, disrupted proceedings by yawning, checking his watch and loudly snoring during the twenty-minute induction speech read by France's culture minister. The audience roared. Culture minister Renaud Donnedieu de Vabres clutched his speech to his chest as Lewis tried to grab it and told the crowd, "The longer my remarks last the better, so you can keep on enjoying Jerry Lewis's comic talents."

Yeah. Right.

It's confusing. This is a nation that gave the world Notre Dame Cathedral, René Descartes, Versailles, champagne and Edith Piaf. They are a subtle, multilayered, transcendentally metaphysical people. Is it conceivable that the French see something in America's most cornball comedian that escapes the rest of us?

Jerry Lewis?

Sois sérieuse, chérie. Ce n'est pas possible.

Generalissimo Franco is Still Dead

There's a famous poem by Shelley concerning the remains of a massive statue of an ancient king found in the Egyptian desert. On the pedestal was an inscription that read, "My name is Ozymandias, King of Kings. Look upon my works, ye mighty, and despair!" Shelley notes that aside from the pedestal all that could be seen were "Two vast and trunkless legs . . . near them, half sunk, a shattered visage lies . . . "

So much for the King of Kings' staying power. Recently I was reminded of Ozymandias and monarchical hubris by a small item tucked away on page twenty-four of my newspaper. The headline read, "Madrid's Last Franco Statue is Removed." That would be Generalissimo Francisco Franco, a sour Galician military opportunist who, in the midthirties, overthrew Spain's elected government and plunged his country into a bloody civil war that cost the lives of nearly four hundred thousand Spaniards.

Franco was short and pudgy with black button eyes and a comic bottle-brush moustache that made him look like a not-terribly-successful door-to-door salesman. He was in fact a ruthless SOB who showed no mercy and took damn few prisoners. Franco so loved his fellow countrymen that he allowed Hitler to use a defenceless Basque village as bombing practice for the German Luftwaffe. On the afternoon of April 27, 1937, Junkers bombers pounded the hamlet with high-explosive and incendiary bombs in the middle of market day when it was most crowded. German Heinkel fighters strafed the townsfolk as they ran into the fields to escape the bombs. Sixteen hundred unarmed peasants were killed or wounded. The town—Guernica—burned for three days.

Franco was unrepentant. He expressed his political philosophy quite succinctly. "Our regime," he explained, "is based on bayonets and blood, not on hypocritical elections."

I lived in Spain in the late sixties, a quarter-century after the fighting stopped. Spanish citizens were still wary. Guardia Civil officers, with their goofy patent-leather hats and not-so-goofy submachine guns, were everywhere. So, I was assured, were government spies. Politics were not discussed around strangers.

On the twenty-fifth anniversary of the war's end, a mildly satirical Spanish magazine published an issue, the cover of which bore the legend "Veinti-Cinco Años de Paz y Sciencia"—which translates as "twenty-five years of peace and science." But if you say it fast in Spanish, it translates as "twenty-five years of . . . patience."

The people I was staying with predicted that the magazine would be shut down and the editor would be jailed.

Franco died in 1975. In his own bed, unfortunately, instead of in the jail cell where he belonged. He spent the last four decades of his life as "El Caudillo"—the leader—of a nation still traumatized by its awful civil war. He ruled with an iron fist and a grim determination that Spain would remain backward and insular. And it did—until he died.

Whereupon Spain began to carefully but deliberately join the twentieth century.

I'm sure such an eventuality never occurred to Franco. I have no doubt that "the general of generals" took it for granted that the Spain he left behind would never flirt with that seductive stranger, democracy, and the name Franco would resonate reverentially in the annals of Spanish history forever.

Resonate, maybe, but not reverentially. Within three years of his death, Spain had a new and democratic constitution, and the legacy of Franco was already being dismantled brick by brick.

In the Spain I knew, Franco's portrait hung in every classroom and public gathering place. There were statues of him everywhere. Today there is just one left in the city of Santander, and that city's mayor has announced that it, too, will be removed.

As for the Madrid statue—a larger-than-life bronze depicting Franco on horseback—it was dismantled and trucked to a warehouse. Not without incident. Hundreds of Franco loyalists jeered and gave the fascist salute as the statue was removed. But a spokesman for the government said the action was taken because "the statue was not appreciated by a majority of the people."

Debate has now begun on what should fill the vacuum left in the San Juan de la Cruz plaza where the statue stood.

I dunno. How about a sculpture of two trunkless legs and a half-sunk shattered visage?

BODY LANGUAGE

Have a Nice Day

I have spent an excessive amount of time and energy loathing the phrase "Have a nice day." Four simple, one-syllable words shouldn't have the power to get under my skin, but they do, partly because I hear them so much. The guy at the gas pump says them to me. So does the grocery checkout clerk. I get the same mumbled benediction from the bank teller and my doctor's receptionist. I'd no doubt hear it from the butcher, the baker and the candlestick maker, if I did business with them.

Have a nice day. The only satisfying retort I ever heard to that phrase came from the lips of humourist Russell Baker. When a car salesman urged him to have a nice day, Baker snapped, "No thanks. I've made other plans."

Have a nice day. So bland, so meaningless.

Well, meaningless to me. I imagine Ted Fink would give his right hand to have just one nice day.

No, strike that. He's already given most of his right hand. And his nose. And his ears. And pretty much all of the skin on his body.

That sort of thing can happen when a four-thousand-litre propane tank blows up in your face.

The accident occurred on Ted Fink's thousand-hectare farm in Illinois back in 1999. Fink was driving his John Deere, moving the tank across the barnyard, when a chain holding the tank snapped. The tank broke loose, tumbled to the ground and sprang a leak. The escaping propane must have been ignited by a spark. Neighbours on a farm almost two kilometres away from the Fink spread felt the thump of the explosion. When Ted's wife Rhoda got to the barnyard, all she saw was a giant ball of flame. Ted Fink was somewhere in the middle of it.

He woke up eight months later in the burn unit of the University of Wisconsin hospital. A miracle? No doubt. A blessing? That's less clear. Ted Fink had suffered hideous burns to ninety-three percent of his body. Doctors originally calculated the likelihood of his dying at 138 percent. He survived, but "survive" was the operative word. His hair was gone, as were the thumb, index and middle finger of his right hand. His ears burned right off, as did most of his nose. The rest of him was pretty much a mass of scar tissue.

Gone also was the cheery, bustling, hard-working farmer who scampered up silo ladders, sprinted across fields and manhandled hay bales as if they were couch pillows. The new Ted Fink couldn't walk from the ambulance to his house. He had to relearn things like holding a knife and fork. Rhoda had to dress him and get him in and out of the shower. All he wanted to do was sleep.

The internal story wasn't any cheerier. As a result of his accident and multiple surgeries, his joints became inflamed and fused with bone. He can't lift his grandchildren onto his lap. His legs now are permanently bent, which means he can't lie flat in bed. He sleeps in a recliner in the living room. And his new "skin" is giving him grief. It's tough and crusty, and it's shrivelling. The skin on his neck is tightening, pulling his lower lip downward so that he can no longer close his mouth fully. He could go back to the hospital for further surgery, but Ted Fink's had enough of scalpels and skin grafts. His energy has come back some, and he gets out on the tractor now and again to help his son, who has taken over the running of the farm. Ted still keeps the books.

Does Ted Fink sometimes wish he'd just died that day in the barnyard? If he does, he doesn't let on. And he showed his appreciation for his wife Rhoda's devotion by buying her a diamond ring after he got home from the hospital.

Ted Fink lives in a world of disfigurement and pain—but he lives. And he gets to see his son Chris work the same farm that five generations of Finks worked before him. And he gets to hold his grandchildren in his lap, even if another adult has to put them there.

He also gets to serve as an object lesson for ungrateful clods like yours truly. Next time somebody tells me to have a nice day, I intend to take that advice.

Hey, Big Guy,
Got a Macho?

When I lived in Madrid, I occasionally took in a bullfight. The Spanish *corrida* is a lavish spectacle, consisting for the most part of glittering, skittering men dodging angry, snorting beasts that look like runaway locomotives with horns.

The bulls are magnificent in their sleek, primal brutishness.

The bullfighters . . . not so much.

Your average *torero* looks like a Boy George wet dream. Pink cape? Skin-tight satin trousers? Mouseketeer hat and ballet slippers? Come on.

What's even more disconcerting for the average North American is the average bullfighter's, um, basket.

Or as my companion at the last bullfight I attended somewhat tactlessly put it, "Hey! Has El Dominguín got a *teacup* in his pants?"

Could be. Bullfighters are notorious for enhancing their manhood with handkerchiefs, paper towels, mangos or anything else they can stuff down their front. It's a melodramatic attempt to heighten what's on the line, as it were. Here's a guy willing to place his (admittedly half-fake) bulge perilously close to the trajectory of razor sharp horns attached to eight hundred kilos of galloping, murderous bull.

Makes a fella cross his legs just to think about it—and it makes a woman shake her head. One more stupid guy trick. Well, it's not our fault, ladies. You've probably noticed that guys just don't think all that clearly when it comes to Mr. Happy and The Twins. Which might help to explain what's happening these days at Santa Maria Nuova Hospital in Florence, Italy. They're admitting a lot of male tourists, usually unconscious, though occasionally raving. These chaps have one thing in common: they were all in the Accademia Gallery standing in front of Michelangelo's statue of David when they flipped out.

Transfixed by the sheer aesthetic beauty of the piece? Dr. Graziella Magherini thinks not. She's been studying these victims of what she calls "panic attacks" for the past year and she's concluded the men were overwhelmed by feelings of inadequacy.

Not surprising, really. Michelangelo's David stands about five metres tall. That means David's *Signor Felice* must be at least . . . well, you do the math.

A lot of marble is all I'm saying.

Other signs of penile hysteria abound. Did you know there's an obscure branch of Kung Fu dedicated to extreme penis feats? It's called Jiu Jiu Shen Gong and it's become popular enough to generate its own video, which I hope never to see. It's enough to know that a Jiu Jiu Shen Gong practitioner in Hong Kong claims to have achieved sufficient mastery of technique to be able to lift a seventy-five-kilogram barbell using only his penis.

Which is something else I don't wish to see.

And that goes double for the guy who rigged his rig to a truck bumper in a parking lot in Fremont, California, and managed to haul the vehicle several metres before, I presume, bursting into an aria from *Figaro.* You can view the feat, if you're so inclined, in a BBC-TV documentary entitled, appropriately enough, *Penis Envy.*

Or if you want to elevate to a higher plane, you could visit the town of Chucuito, high in the mountains of Peru. There you can view twenty-four 1.5 metre tall phalluses carved out of stone more than five hundred years ago by ancient Incan artisans. Thousands of tourists have made the trek to visit Peru's penis patch.

Proving that if (as P.T. Barnum opined) there's a sucker born every minute, a significant percentage of them take their vacations in Peru. Archeologists investigating the "shrine" recently determined that the "erections" were actually erected in 1993 by local stone masons employed by the Chucuito Chamber of Commerce.

Just another stupid guy trick.

It's the reason men have never been mistaken for Canada Savings Bonds. Because at some point, savings bonds mature.

Hands Off My Hands

Why do you figure Michael Jackson wears that white glove so much? I think I know. I think it's because the hand that's in the glove is close to half a century old and beginning to look it. And Michael Jackson, a.k.a. The Neverland Kid, simply couldn't stand the rest of the world knowing that his hands look old.

He's not the only one trying desperately to turn back the biological clock. Hair dyes and wrinkle creams are selling as never before. Wave after wave of new diet fads wash over the populace. You see people signing up for Pilates and Tai Chi lessons. Jumping in the pool for Aquafit classes. Wheezing around gymnasiums with their fellow aerobics fanatics.

All in an effort to slam the door on Father Time.

And then there's the knife. In 2003, US surgeons performed nine *million* cosmetic surgeries, from Botox injections to liposuction, not forgetting chemical peels, dermabrasion and microphlebectomy— which is a fancy word for stripping out varicose veins. Fountain of Youth pursuers are getting their lips inflated and their bums trimmed, their boobs fluffed up and their tummies sanded down. Not to mention ear tucks, eyelid nips and extra-chin removals.

The latest surgical fad? The hand job, so to speak. Folks are lining up for "handlifts." The reconstructive procedure removes liver spots and injects fat cells to smooth out wrinkles on the customers' hands. A proper handlift will set you back somewhere between five and six grand, depending on the toniness of your surgeon or specialist.

And you'll need to hire someone to turn the pages of *Vanity Fair* for you while you're recovering—it can take six months for the hands to "settle," as cosmeticians say. Even then there might be a teensy-weensy bit of scarring to contend with.

And oh yes, you'll need to check in with your surgeon for a wee tune-up—more injections, possibly some colour adjustments—every six months or so.

But hey—look at the upside. You come out of it with hands as smooth and soft as a prepubescent's posterior. Why, those hands will look like they belong to an eighteen-year-old mademoiselle of leisure.

Might seem a little incongruous if they're attached to the blubbery arms of a bewattled senior citizen, but what the hell—wear long sleeves.

Or not. My hands are even older—and older looking—than Michael Jackson's, but I'm kind of fond of them. For one thing they are indisputably my hands and nobody else's. There's that purple seam that runs across my right index finger between the first and second knuckles. Picked that up opening a can of dog food back when I was a pup. My left thumb is still crooked from that time four or five decades ago when I pitched off a toboggan and jammed it into the frozen turf, and one of my knuckles bears a dime-sized scar from a clumsy fist fight way back in grade eleven.

And then, of course, there are the wrinkles. My hands have more seams and creases than an unironed bedspread, but I don't mind. I earned those wrinkles packing snowballs and paddling canoes, pounding nails and washing dishes. I like my hands just the way they are.

But they're not the most impressive set of dukes I ever saw. Those belong to a senior citizen brother-in-law of mine whose hands have done more things in this life than most. And they show it. They are big and red and beefy. They don't look like the kind of hands you would find hoisting a Wedgwood china teacup or conducting a symphony orchestra. Nevertheless they are a spectacular pair of paws. Here's what his daughter Adrienne wrote about her father's hands:

> His hands have always fascinated me . . . they have built homes to shelter family and friends, held every tool imaginable with confidence and skill, tinkered cold, silent engines to life and knuckle-danced their way across countless kitchen tables to entertain a mesmerized child.
>
> With fingers like thick sausages and the grip of a grizzly, his handshake reveals the strength and integrity that define his utter being. His hands are the book of his life. Their wrinkles and blisters, their nicks and scars are the words in his wonderful tale.

Michael Jackson, eat your heart out.

Laugh? I Thought I'd Diet

A re you fat? I am.

Not grotesquely fat. I don't get mistaken for the Graf Zeppelin. I don't look like the Michelin Man or Pavarotti. We're not talking Orson Welles North here. But fat. Fatter than I want to be. Fatter than I ought to be. About eleven kilograms heavier than I was the last time my back didn't ache and my knees didn't hurt.

And I know exactly who to blame it on—that chubby guy in the mirror.

It's such a bummer, being fat. It sneaks up on you, one eggnog at a time. All those second helpings. The sour cream on the potatoes. The bagels, the Turtles, the extra pats of butter. That irresistible burger with fries. That "impulse" Crispy Crunch at the checkout counter. Suddenly (well, not so suddenly) there you are.

Fat.

There are solutions, of course. Bookstores are full of them. There's the Pritikin Diet and Dr. Atkins' Diet Revolution, not to mention the South Beach diet, the Grapefruit Diet, the cabbage soup diet and even, I swear, the submarine sandwich diet.

There's just the one small drawback with all these diet fads. They don't work. Not for most of us, anyway. Because they are all too boring or annoying or expensive or complicated, and most of us creep back to our old lifestyles and the bad diet that got us throwing our money away on diet books in the first place.

So what do we do? Have gastrointestinal bypass surgery? Sew our lips together? Actually there's a much cheaper and simpler solution that would work perfectly for about ninety-eight percent of us fatties. We just need to keep our mouth shut more often.

The simple truth is, we eat too much. Dr. Black's Diet Revolution: Eat less, lose weight.

You're welcome.

Actually, I have another diet tip that might help: the story of Patrick Deuel.

Mr. Deuel is a resident of Valentine, Nebraska. He is forty-two years old. Last summer he was admitted to the Avera McKennan Hospital in Sioux Falls, South Dakota, in grave condition, suffering from diabetes and heart failure.

Why heart failure in such a relatively young guy? Doctors attributed his medical condition directly to Mr. Deuel's body mass index. He was fat. Really fat.

Four hundred and eighty-six kilograms fat.

That is more than a full-grown horse and just a bit less than a mature pilot whale. Patrick Deuel weighed more than twice as much as a fully loaded Harley-Davidson Sportster.

Patrick Deuel was so obese that he hadn't been able to get out of his house for seven years. In fact, for more than half a year he hadn't even been able to get out of bed. When they got him to the hospital Mr. Deuel was too far gone for the gastric bypass surgery they thought he needed, so hospital dieticians put him on a strict regimen of twelve hundred calories a day. That's less than one supersized Big Mac meal.

Mr. Deuel rallied, and the bypass surgery was performed successfully last October. Recently there was a newspaper photograph of the man walking across the Avera McKennan hospital lobby.

Sort of.

He is supporting himself on two aluminum walkers. He is wearing running shoes, sweat pants and a tee shirt. He is barely recognizable as a human being. His torso is bulging, his belly distended and sagging almost to his knees. He has giant fat rolls on his *back.*

Even his elbows have double chins.

But what's really sobering is—this is the *new* Patrick Deuel. After he's shed a mind-blowing two hundred kilograms.

He's now down to a svelte 277 kilograms and hopes (some day) to bottom out at around 110 kilos.

I wish him luck and I owe him big time. He's a personal inspiration to me.

I've put that newspaper photo of Patrick Deuel where I figure it will do me the most good.

Scotch-taped to my refrigerator door.

Too Dumb to Live

I remember the first (and last) time I ever went into a Playboy Club. It was in New York City, back in the eighties. Like many another boomer, I had spent a lot of my teen years with well-thumbed copies of *Playboy Magazine* under my mattress. Come adulthood, I'd stopped actually buying the rag, but somewhere in the recesses of my crocodile mind, I still thought of the whole Playboy lifestyle as vaguely hip and cool.

So I went into the Playboy Club in lower Manhattan and ordered an overpriced cocktail, and what did I see around me?

Geeks. Nerds. Big-time losers. Fat guys wearing bad suits and worse toupees leering at women dressed in fishnet stockings and bunny suits. Cottontails with cleavage.

That's when it first dawned on me. Males—maybe we're too dumb to live.

And not just human-type males. Consider an obnoxious little member of the *Empididae* family known as the dance fly. This winged denizen of Australia has been observed flitting up to female dance flies with pieces of junk that he presents as "tokens of appreciation." While the gal is oohing and aahing over his thoughtfulness, he's Having His Way with her. By the time the female discovers she's been had, in more ways then one, the male has taken off to look for a new conquest.

If that isn't Hugh Hefner in action, I'll eat my Viagra prescription.

Then there's the primate known as the *rhesus macaque.* This monkey's even more . . . male. A team of zoologists from Duke University has found that the male macaque is willing to give up food in exchange for being permitted to view photographs of female monkeys' bottoms.

Giving up lunch to gawk at centrefolds. Reminds me of a pimply school kid I once—er, knew.

Moving up (?) to *Homo sapiens,* we see even more evidence that males aren't getting any smarter. I'm no zoologist, but you don't have to be David Suzuki to figure out that mass self-mutilation is a sure sign of species distress. Once again male humans are sending out an SOS. Doctors are noticing a staggering upsurge in emergency room crises involving male handymen.

Amateur handymen, it should be added. These are the guys who get a circular saw from their kids for Father's Day and proceed to crosscut their pinkie fingers off because they really don't know what they're doing.

And it's not just power saws. Hapless do-it-yourselfers are filleting themselves with chain saws, amputating their toes with power mowers, tumbling off ladders, whoopsy-daisying off roofs, staple-gunning their thumbs to the wallboard and flash-barbecuing themselves while messing with their home wiring system.

Dr. Mark Roper, director of the division of primary care at McGill University in Montreal, just shakes his head.

"People—read 'men'—are just not paying attention when they're pushing the wood across the saw," he says. "We also see eye injuries because they're not wearing eye protection."

Notice how diplomatically he avoids the word "dumb"?

Speaking of "dumb" and "men"—how about an honorary dunce cap for Canadian Fred Gilliland? Fred doesn't seem to be a dumb guy at first glance. As a matter of fact he seems pretty shrewd. Shrewd enough, US authorities say, to have scammed twenty-nine million dollars out of gullible American investors back in 1999.

And shrewd enough to scuttle back across the Canadian border just ahead of the feds to live in luxury in Vancouver while fighting extradition back to the States.

Not quite shrewd enough, however, to outwit one of his fraud victims, who pulled a "bygones will be bygones" routine on Gilliland, chatted him up like an old pal and invited him to lunch just across the border in Point Roberts, Washington.

The draw? "C'mon Fred . . . I know this restaurant that's got a two-for-one lunch special on Wednesdays."

Gilliland bit. The border guards, who had been tipped off, let him into the States without a hassle. FBI agents were waiting at the back of the restaurant.

Once he was in handcuffs, Gilliland's "pal" smiled at him and said, "Cheer up, Fred. Now you've got 3,650 free lunches coming to you."

Hey Fred—ever heard of the dance fly?

The Shoes We Choose . . .

Remember leather shoes? There was a time not so very long ago when every middle-class North American male past puberty routinely crammed his feet into a pair of nonbreathing, arch-crushing, toe-mangling leather shoes every morning as a matter of course. Nowadays? Check out the feet of the next ten males you pass on the street. Unless you're at a funeral, a wedding or on Bay Street, I'll betcha eight of them are wearing some variation of what Canucks are pleased to call the running shoe. I say hallelujah and good riddance. Those leather shoes of yesteryear were an abomination on mankind.

My old man wore leather shoes his whole working life. And each workday evening after dinner he stuck his aching dogs in a basin full of hot water and Epsom salts to soothe the bunions and corns caused by his lousy footwear. As far as I'm concerned, running shoes (sneakers to Americans) are the best thing to happen to men's pedal extremities since Madame LaZonga's Erotic Foot Massage.

Of course they're misnamed. Most of us who wear them seldom run and hardly ever sneak. And yes, they're garish and ungainly looking, but Lordy, they're kind to the tootsies.

That said, there is the danger of Too Much of a Good Thing.

Such a situation seemed to be playing out in San Francisco recently, where footwear fetishists lined up *for an entire week* in front of a store called Niketown for the privilege of laying down US$295 per person just to buy one pair of running shoes.

Not just any running shoes, mind you—Air Jordan VI Retro basketball shoes.

So were these eerily patient shoe seekers merely netball wannabes? Aspiring athletes looking for some hi-tech gear to help them crash the NBA? Nope. They call themselves "sneakerheads." They had no intention of ever actually, you know, *wearing* the shoes they were so desperate to buy. They simply collect them, like foreign stamps or rare coins. As one sneakerhead explained to *San Francisco Chronicle* reporter Steven Rubenstein, "Wearing them would be stupid. If you wear them, the value goes down real fast. They get creases in them."

So what is the point?

"They express your personality," says another sneakerhead. "They speak up for you without words. They say you're hip, that you're not a follower. These shoes tell you who you are."

What I've always craved—a pair of shoes to tell me who I am.

Some people take their sneakers dead seriously. A kid in Philadelphia was shot and killed for his Air Jordans a few years back. Same thing happened to a guy in Houston in 1996.

But perhaps the most bizarre sneaker story comes from the Mexican-American border where the coolest thing you can slip your feet into these days is a pair of Brincos.

Brincos—the name comes from the Spanish word for jump—are at least as specialized as Air Jordan VI Retros—but not for the game of basketball. Unlike the typically lurid running shoe, Brincos are dark for camouflage. They also feature unusually high ankle support, for negotiating treacherous terrain by night.

In fact they come with a host of oddball accoutrements—a built-in miniature compass, a clip-on miniflashlight, plus a tiny pocket for painkillers—all of which sounds unusual, but is as nothing compared to one more strange feature you won't find with any other running shoe.

Pull out the insole of a Brinco and you're looking at a detailed, full-colour map of southwestern North America—specifically, the best route to take from Tijuana, Mexico, to San Diego, California.

So who's likely to want a pair of Brincos? A very specific group—border hoppers. Latin Americans eager to enter the USA by the back door, without benefit of passport or green card.

Sounds like way too small a target group until you crunch the numbers. The US Border Patrol estimates that 14.7 million Latinos were involved in "illegal crossovers" between 1990 and the year 2000. And the numbers are growing.

On the other hand, people willing to risk their lives sneaking past rattlesnakes, Mexican banditos and trigger-happy US border patrollers probably don't have a whole lot of discretionary income. Are they likely to lash out US$215 for a pair of Brincos?

Sounds more like a PR stunt to me. And indeed Judi Werthein, who created the Brincos, describes them as more of an artistic statement than simple footwear. She says they show "how a product can mean different things in different economies."

At the very least, Brincos bring a whole new relevance to the term "sneakers."

Take It Off, Eh?

How idiotic civilization is! Why be given a body if you
have to shut it up in a case, like a rare, rare fiddle?
—KATHERINE MANSFIELD

I expect Sharon Smith would agree with that fashion statement.

Ms. Smith—make that Mayor Smith; she became the first female mayor of her town when the citizens of Houston, BC, elected her a couple of years ago—celebrated her ascension to office by posing for an official photograph. It shows her in the mayor's chambers, sitting in the mayor's chair, wearing her shiny new chain of office, a radiant smile . . .

And nothing else.

Which would have been a fine and private joke between the mayor and her photographer husband, had not some unnamed party guest discovered the photos on the Smith home computer, downloaded them onto a CD and subsequently cast them across the internet for the rest of the world to see.

Outrageous behaviour? Perhaps by the standards of the Houston citizenry, but the notion of going to work in the buff isn't all that radical in other environs. Two flight attendants with Southwest Airlines were recently nonplussed upon responding to an inflight summons from the cockpit of their Boeing 747. "Bring some paper napkins and soda water," they were told. They went to the cockpit and found the pilot and the co-pilot at the controls, wearing their headphones, big grins . . .

And nothing else.

Back in the dot-com glory days of the late eighties, one computer programmer was famous throughout the length of the Silicon Valley. The man was a cyber genius. Every major player from Microsoft down was itching to hire him. He could name his own price, and he did. Forget the megabucks, stock options or candy-apple red Porsche in the parking lot. His non-negotiable clause: he insisted on working in the nude.

So his company let him. Mind you, they put him on the night shift, solo, and kept the blinds down, but still . . .

There was a brief moment in the dwindling years of the last century when it looked like corporate drones everywhere might one day shuck their pinstripes in favour of birthday suits. In her book *Work Naked*, which was published a few years back, author Cynthia Froggatt argued that it was high time the traditional workplace was overhauled from top to bottom—including employees going topless and bottomless, if that worked for them.

Alas, it didn't. The Back-to-Basics Labour-in-the-Raw movement fizzled faster than a popsicle in a steam bath.

That naked cybergeek genius programmer in Silicon Valley? He freaked out a fellow employee, who complained to security, and security made him put on some clothes—at gunpoint.

Those bare-bottomed Southwest Airlines sky jockeys? They claimed that they'd splashed some coffee on their uniforms and taken them off to clean them, but the flight attendants didn't buy it, and neither did their bosses at Southwest Airlines. The naked flyboys have been permanently grounded.

Turns out that most folks aren't all that crazy about the idea of toiling in the buff—or about working next to colleagues similarly unattired. And I have to say I agree with them. Of all the people I worked beside down the years, I saw more than enough of their naked essence from the neck up—and I dare say they felt the same way about me.

Mind you, I spent most of my working years with the Canadian Broadcasting Corporation, where the idea of a formal dress code was about as foreign as pork chops at a bar mitzvah. If your ratings were good, CBC honchos didn't care if you showed up for work in a rhinestone thong and a Batman cape.

Now that I'm retired from the nine-to-five and scribbling in comfort out of my own house, the dress code is even more relaxed. Hugh Hefner spent his working years cranking out *Playboy Magazine* while dressed in silk pajamas?

I've got that beat.

Sitting here, typing out the final words of this column, I happen to be wearing . . .

Well, you probably don't want to know.

But Mayor Smith would appreciate it.

Should You Smoke After Sex?

When I was young, ashtrays were everywhere and the entire damn male world smoked like coal-fired locomotives. Bogie and Eastwood, Churchill and Edward R. Murrow, Dad and my uncles, one hundred percent of all the cool guys in my class and several of the dorks like myself. Smoking was hip. It was sexy. Smoking was, as humourist Fran Leibowitz so eloquently put it, the whole point of being a grown-up.

Times change and so do tastes. You still see smokers up on the big screen, but check out who's actually sucking on the butts these days.

It's not heroes like Humphrey and Clint. It's doofuses, low-lifes and also-rans. Sean Penn as murderer-rapist Matthew Poncelet in *Dead Man Walking.* Tony Sirico as dim-bulb hit man Paulie "Walnuts" Gaultieri in *The Sopranos.*

This is not my imagination. It's official. Researchers participating in a study conducted at St. Michael's Medical Center in Newark, New Jersey, sat through 447 Hollywood movies, all the top-ten box office hits since 1990 that dealt with contemporary American society.

Observations: nearly forty percent of the bad guys had nicotine habits compared with just twenty percent of the good guys. And almost fifty percent of the smokers were portrayed as members of "lower socio-economic classes."

Clearly Hollywood is engaged in some serious message sending here, and the message is: Smoking is for losers.

And if the message is getting less subtle, so are the messengers. A recent production of Arthur Miller's play *A View from the Bridge* ground to a halt when a woman in the audience stood up and screamed at the stage, "Put out that cigarette!"

The smoking actor, Sebastiano Lo Monaco, was dumbfounded. "This has never happened to me in more than 300 performances," the actor . . . er, fumed. The performance was suspended for fifteen minutes, and then resumed with an "amended" script featuring a suddenly smoke-free protagonist.

Did I mention that this incident occurred in a theatre in Rome, Italy—where smoking has been a sacred rite among Italian men since Nero went around igniting Christians? No more. For the past year it's been illegal to light up in any enclosed public place in the entire country.

The tobacco worm has turned, and not just in Italy. Non-smokers rule! And any poor wretch still chained to his Marlboros can expect nothing but scorn, ridicule . . .

And photographic revisionism. Consider the classic children's book *Goodnight Moon* by Margaret Wise Brown. It's sold millions of copies, most of them with a photograph of the illustrator, Clement Hurd, on the back cover. There is Hurd, looking cheerful and relaxed, smiling back at the camera.

With an unmistakable cigarette between the first two fingers of his right hand.

The outrage couldn't stand, of course, and it hasn't. Any copy of *Goodnight Moon* you find in bookstores now still features Mr. Hurd on the back cover, but the cigarette in his hand has artfully "disappeared," airbrushed into oblivion.

The publisher, HarperCollins, said it altered the photo to avoid giving "the appearance of encouraging smoking." What next? Will the publishers who put out the autobiography of the Dalai Lama paint hats on the front cover photos of His Holiness to avoid giving the appearance of encouraging baldness?

And what of other famous smokers in history? Will General MacArthur wade ashore without his corncob pipe? Will pictures of FDR no longer show him smiling perkily, a gasper jammed in a long-stemmed cigarette holder clamped between his teeth? Will we see Groucho Marx without a cigar?

It all sounds way too much like those famous photos of the Soviet Politburo in Stalin's time. Joe was a poster boy for Tony Soprano. Every time somebody bugged him, Joe had him whacked—or relocated to East Iceberg, Siberia. And in the next officially circulated Soviet government group photo, you would see this airy space where Comrade Igor Fallguy used to be.

Now we're using the same technique on cigarette smokers, and nobody complains. I doubt anybody will stand in the path of the juggernaut non-smokers' lobby. Smoking is passé and isn't likely to ever swim back into favour.

Pity. It leaves behind some unanswered questions. Such as the one posed in the headline to this column: Should you smoke after sex?

According to Woody Allen, the answer is no. He says if you smoke after sex, you're doing it too fast.

Beauty is Only Scalpel Deep

At 50, everyone has the face he deserves.
—GEORGE ORWELL

Oh yeah? Well, don't try to tell that to Joan Rivers, George. The acid-tongued comedienne is into her seventy-second year—and hiding behind her umpty-eleventh face lift.

She started having her mug remodelled back in 1965, when she had a couple of satchels of unsolicited luggage excised from underneath her eyes. In the following forty years she has had: her cheekbones elevated, her ears sculpted, her brow sanded smooth, her chin trimmed back, her neck wattles ironed flat and her nose whittled down 'til it's almost as nonexistent as Michael Jackson's.

And it's not over yet. Joan Rivers's puss is a work in progress. She still pops into her friendly cosmetologist every four months for Botox injections and collagen treatments. She is basically a fleshy fraud; an architectural fake from the neck up.

And she's damn proud of it.

"I have become," she says, "the poster girl for plastic surgery." Why does she do it? "Number one," she says briskly, "when you look better you are treated differently. Number two: people want to be around attractive people."

Planet Earth to Joan:

Number one: If you're hanging around with folks who give you thumbs up or down depending on your wrinkle quotient, you need to upgrade to a classier circle of friends.

And number two: Sorry kiddo, but all that pain and all that stitch work have not left you looking all that attractive. On my TV you look like an X-ray of a scarecrow. In close-ups your head looks like a cartoon face sketched on a nylon stocking stretched over a light bulb.

You look . . . weird.

Which is not to say Joan Rivers is the most outlandish living example of cosmetic surgery gone nuts. Michael Jackson's got her whupped in that department. And a walking nightmare named Jocelyn Wildenstein leaves them both in the dust. (Check her out at www.awfulplasticsurgery.com—if you dare.)

Like Wildenstein and Jackson, Joan Rivers continues to pursue her doomed quest to recage the sweet bird of youth. "It's an obligation," she says. As for those who laugh at her, Ms. Rivers responds with a dismissive snort: "They cannot parody you unless they know you, and when they know you, it means you're part of the culture, it means you're successful."

Yeah, well, Frankenstein, Godzilla and The Incredible Hulk are all part of the culture too. But I don't see anybody submitting to the surgeon's scalpel to try and look like them.

It makes you want to take Joan Rivers by the shoulders, look her in the eye and say, "Joan, you are seventy-two years old. It's okay to have wrinkles. You've earned them."

Nobody ever had wrinkles to match the English poet, Wystan Hugh Auden. He was only sixty-six when he died, but his face looked eons older. He once observed, "My face looks like a wedding cake left out in the rain."

Naw. His face was beautiful. It looked like a contour map of the backside of the moon, all stress lines and laugh creases and sad furrows. It was magnificent—the road map of his well-lived life. Why would he not want his face to reflect who he was? What is it that's come undone in our culture that moves so many to shell out megabucks and endure carloads of pain so they can have a face as surreally smooth as a baby's bum?

At the risk of sounding corny, it really is what's inside, not outside, that counts. Paul Bernardo had a baby face; Sir John A. MacDonald's mug looked like forty kilometres of bad road. Who would you rather have in your lifeboat?

Enjoy yourself. Laugh much. Allow your life to show in your face. And remember the words of Oregon artist and poet Anthony Euwer:

> As a beauty, I'm not a great star.
> There are others more handsome by far.
> But my face—I don't mind it
> Because I'm behind it;
> It's the folks out in front that I jar.

My Back Story

Amazing how one's life can change with the flip of a card, a roll of the dice, a shift of the wind.

Or a simple bend from the waist.

There I was, standing in the front hall to go through the mail, when a personal letter from Ed McMahon slipped through my fingers and fell at my feet. Well, I thought, I'll just bend down and pi—

AAAAAAAARRRRRGGGGGGHHHHH!

Threw my back out. Specifically, my portside sacroiliac joint, according to the chiropractor Lynne bundled me off to consult. It wouldn't be so galling if I'd been humping hay bales up into a barn loft, arm wrestling Don Cherry or trying to haul a bull calf out of a bog, but I was picking up an envelope, for God's sake. And in a micromoment I went from being a robust, able-bodied mature male to a semi-crippled sack of stricken protoplasm.

Bad backs are no fun—and they darken the horizons of more than the sufferer. There's a pretty good chance that for the last couple of years of his life, the thirty-fifth president of the United States, John Fitzgerald Kennedy, cursed under his breath every time he heard the word "Canada."

That would be a consequence of JFK's visit to Ottawa back in 1961. Prime Minister John Diefenbaker, pooh-poohing the advice of nervous White House staff, arranged for the President to plant a ceremonial maple tree in front of Rideau Hall. A young, vibrant Kennedy, already less than enamoured of his host and of the chore, decided to get it over with quickly. He leaned into his ceremonial spade, hefted a huge clod of earth and . . .

AAAAAAAARRRRRGGGGGGHHHHH!

Aggravated an old wartime injury. JFK spent the rest of his life suffering from chronic back pain, the only relief from which he found in a rocking chair that he kept in the Oval Office.

For me, leadership of the western world has never been a serious option, but even in my limited sphere, I've been surprised how severely my life has been circumscribed just because of a wonky hinge in the middle of my carcass. Slippers, loafers and moccasins become the only viable footwear, because there's no way I'm going to get down and tie laces. Anything dropped on the floor stays on the floor until someone else (Lynne, most likely) comes along to pick it up. Simply getting out of bed in the morning is a five-minute operation that involves whimpering and moaning while scuttling across the mattress like a bottom-feeding crustacean, then hanging on to Lynne while I haul myself vertical.

And there are few experiences quite as humbling as having to call out, "Honey? Could you help me with my underpants?"

But there's an upside to having a bad back, especially if you're an inherently lazy sod like me. The garbage cans will wait another week. The lawn will remain unmowed for the foreseeable future. In fact, all manual chores, from watering plants to walking the dog, are pretty much on hold—or on Lynne—until I get the all-clear from the doctor, the chiropractor and the physiotherapist. And it's a great time to catch up on my reading because the only physical position that's truly pain-free turns out to be flat out on my back in bed.

Oh darn.

How long can I expect to lie around, reading novels and being waited on hand, foot and sacroiliac?

"Hard to say," says my chiropractor. "Could be another two weeks, even three."

Lynne, my beloved partner, is less pessimistic. She thinks I'll be up and around a lot sooner than that.

Oh, she hasn't said so in so many words, but I can tell.

It's the little things. The muttered curses, the slamming cupboard doors.

The underpants balled up and thrown at my head.

I'm feeling a lot better already.

Fancy Footwear?
What a Croc!

Not long ago I wrote that good old running shoes (sneakers, to our neighbours to the south) were the best thing to happen to the human pedal extremity this side of a barefoot stroll through warm Mississippi mud.

I was mistaken. That honour really goes to Crocs.

They go by other names. Some folks call them jelly shoes. I've also heard them described as Holey Soles, Garden Trolls and even Dawgs Clogs.

All those names describe a recent phenomenon: one-piece slip-on sandals made of a specialized closed-cell resinous foam plastic and available in just about any colour Timothy Leary could imagine. The uppers look like they were caught in a drive-by machine gun attack—they're full of holes that serve as ventilation ports. That's pretty well it for the Croc, design-wise. No laces, no arch supports, no shoe tongues or fancy treads.

Which makes them dirt-cheap as modern footwear goes. If you're a brand-name slave you can pay anywhere from thirty to sixty bucks for a pair of Crocs. I got a pair of knock-offs for $9.95 in a bargain bin at the Real Canadian Superstore.

Even at that, manufacturers must make a killing, considering that a pair of these things consist of nothing more than approximately two bits' worth of moulded plastic.

But the price tag is not the main attraction of Crocs. What's turned this footwear into a hundred-million-dollar-a-year bonanza is the comfort factor. Every step you take with a pair of Crocs on your feet is like a personal foot massage. They are what the Earth Shoe was in the sixties and Birkenstocks were in the seventies—only cheaper and better.

And, it must be said, homelier.

Crocs are butt ugly. They're called Crocs because they look like twin crocodile snouts peeping out from under your pant cuffs. But it's the Cabbage Patch Doll syndrome. Crocs are so abidingly homely that they're kind of loveable. Think Newman on *Seinfeld*. Or maybe Gollum in *Lord of the Rings*.

And people do love them. They've become favourites of hospital workers who have to stand on cold, hard floors all day. Kitchen workers, from chefs to dishwashers, adore them for the same reason. And the appeal of Crocs appears to be near-universal. Country singer Faith Hill appeared on television sporting a pair of Crocs. I knew they'd really arrived the last time I was in Toronto. Walking past the Roots outlet in the Eaton Centre, I noticed that every mannequin in the window was wearing a pair of . . . you guessed it.

Even my brother wears a pair. Orange.

The word is that gardeners love Crocs, but frankly, I don't get that. I wore mine in the garden for about fifteen minutes. The vents in the uppers took in so much soil I felt like Huckleberry Finn.

That said, Crocs are a snap to keep clean—just wash 'em down with the garden hose. Or jump in the lake, if it's nearby. Crocs aren't afraid of a little water. And they float.

Is there a downside to this shoe? Well yeah. They're supposed to be nonslip, but that's not my experience. One afternoon I made the mistake of walking out of a light rain shower and onto the terrazzo floor of a grocery store. It was like stepping onto a raft of banana peels. I was windmilling and pratfalling like Mr. Bean in freefall.

I just missed taking out three shelves of bottled water and a Diet Pepsi display.

I also don't recommend them for hiking. There's zero ankle support and they can twist under your foot in rough terrain. Nor would I suggest walking on a wet deck in Crocs, unless you want to know how Steve Podborski feels when he hits a patch of ice.

But for ordinary, everyday informal wear—when you're not trying to look cool or pick up a date—slip into a pair of Crocs. Your feet have never had it better.

They remind me of a story about the great W.H. Auden. When he was a young and penniless but up-and-coming English writer, someone asked him how his life would be changed if he should one day find himself famous and celebrated.

Auden thought about it for a moment and said, "I believe that I would always wear my carpet slippers."

And so it was, years later, that the Pulitzer Prize winning poet was often seen at black-tie functions decked out in a splendid tuxedo with bow tie and cummerbund. And carpet slippers on his feet.

You just know Auden would have jumped at the chance to wear a pair of Crocs.

Testosterone Always Aims Low

Procter & Gamble, the folks who brought us Mr. Clean, Old Spice and Pampers, have dropped another merchandising cherry bomb in the marketplace.

It's the Intrinsa Patch, an itsy-bitsy flesh-coloured band-aid. P&G hopes most menopausal and post-menopausal women will soon be enthusiastically slapping Intrinsa Patches on their bellies twice a week.

Intrinsa Patch is a testosterone delivery system for females. Now women can partake of the defining chemical compound that animates Iberian fighting bulls, Rottweilers and Don Cherry.

My advice? Run, ladies. Run and hide. This is a roller coaster you don't want to ride.

I speak as an expert. Not on the Intrinsa Patch, but on testosterone in general. I've been mainlining the stuff all my life, and take it from me, it's poison. Nothing but trouble. As Robin Williams said, "There's a design flaw in the human male. God gave us a brain and a penis, but only enough blood to run one at a time."

Testosterone decides which command centre gets the blood. And testosterone always aims low.

The big selling pitch for the Intrinsa Patch is that it will "normalize" the user's sex life. By "normalize," the manufacturers are hinting it will make the user as horny as an eighteen-year-old sailor on shore leave.

But here's a news flash for Procter & Gamble and all the ships at sea: people like you and me *aren't supposed* to be as randy as buccaneers. As mature adults, we've been there, endured that and earned our reward—namely, freedom from around-the-clock lust.

The whole idea of the testosterone patch for women was kick-started by a US study showing nearly half of all post-menopausal women suffer from hypoactive sexual desire disorder. HSDD is defined as a lack of sexual desire causing personal distress.

And how did the authors of this study (sponsored by—*quelle surprise*—Procter & Gamble) divine that nearly half of all women surveyed were "personally distressed" about the state of their sex lives? *Globe and Mail* columnist Margaret Wente wondered about that too. "So far as I can make out," wrote Wente, "they seem to have included every woman who ever had a headache."

Call me cynical, but I hear the distant trill of pharmacy cash registers pinging in three-part harmony. Big Drug's advertising honchos are doing what they do best: inducing consumer anxiety where it didn't exist before—in this case, among mature women.

And why not? They made billions doing the same thing to mature men. Remember life before Viagra? When guys hit fifty, they slowed down a little. We didn't stop having sex; we just stopped obsessing about it. Sometimes we'd even settle for a nap. Or go bowling with the guys instead. Sex didn't disappear; it just went to live where it belongs. In the rumpus room of life.

A lot of us guys felt, frankly, relieved. We even thought we were happy, now that the Leash of Libido had been loosened. But the pharmaceutical industry pronounced us erectily dysfunctional. And they had just the little blue pill to fix the problem, available from your local pharmacy. At prices that would bring a blush of shame to the cheeks of a cocaine dealer.

So now we have the thoroughly depressing spectacle of middle-aged guys popping pills that will allow them to re-enter the rut race and pretend they're not middle-aged at all. Soon to be joined by patch-plastered middle-aged women pretending the same thing.

It's shuck and jive, folks. We don't need this stuff. Grandpa and grandma didn't suffer from hypoactive sexual desire disorder or erectile dysfunction, and neither, I'm betting, do you or I.

Reminds me of a line from a very funny West Coast comedian, Mavis Pickett. Mavis is a rarity among stand-up comedians—a senior citizen. Her on-stage routine is speckled with wry observations about the phenomenon of "getting older."

"Young people are really concerned about what older people think," she purrs into the microphone. "Just the other day, my granddaughter asked me, 'Did you and Grandpa have mutual orgasms?' And I said, 'Well, no dear. We had Metropolitan Life.'"

Sounds like a good policy to me.

Bald is Beautiful

Big news for baldies out of Berlin: scientists claim that, possibly within ten years, male pattern baldness will be a thing of the past.

Canadian researcher Kevin McElwee, who holds a doctoral degree in hair biology (who knew?) told an international meeting of hair research societies that hair cloning is just around the corner. McElwee reckons that if a bald guy has just ten healthy hairs still growing on his head, scientists will soon be able to take follicular cells from those hairs, produce several million cultured cells from them, implant said cells in said guy's scalp, and hey presto! Luxuriant foliage where only windswept arid wastes prevailed.

Thanks all the same, Kevin, but I don't think I'll be lining up for this one. I'm a card-carrying chrome dome who's had a bare upper deck for almost as many years as it was carpeted. And I'm here to tell you that I prefer being bald.

Why is bald better? Let me count the ways.

Number one, less bathroom time. I don't have to juggle cans and tubes of mousse and gel, and I don't have to fuss with hair dryers, brushes or combs. Hell, I can comb what's left of my hair with a damp washcloth.

Secondly, hats. I love hats. I have dozens of them from toques to Tilleys, from berets to Borsalinos. Bald guys get to wear any hat they want any time they like. And unlike our hirsute brethren, we don't have to worry about "hat hair." Nothing looks dopier than that Liberty Bell effect produced when a conspicuously coiffed guy doffs his lid.

Besides, let's face it. Bald is in. Mr. Clean. Mark Messier. Ben Kingsley. Patrick Stewart. Most rap stars and seven-eighths of the beanpoles in the NBA flaunt radiant, weed-free skulls. Bald is so trendy, young studs are shaving their heads to achieve the look it took me decades to perfect.

And I hope you're not still buying the myth that fur on the roof equals fire in the belly? Give me a break. It's time the antiquated notion equating head hair with manliness got deep-sixed. Nothing, actually, could be further from the truth. The fact is, baldness is a sure-fire sign of virility. If you don't believe me, ask some eunuchs. All of them, you might note, sport full heads of hair. There's a reason for that, a biological Catch-22 that all men carry around in their genes. Simply put, there is one, and only one, infallible cure for baldness.

Castration.

The sixty-eight percent of males who will experience significant hair loss before they kick face a brutally simple dilemma. They can keep their testicles or they can keep their pompadours, but they can't have both.

Who says God doesn't have a sense of humour?

Another great thing about baldness. It's a social filtering device, a handy discrimination gauge, like white socks with sandals or hair curlers under a kerchief.

Undisputed fact for men: there are a significant number of women out there who are repulsed, put out or otherwise turned off by guys with thin hair. Undisputed fact number two: unless you're a testosterone-crazed, undiscriminating hump hound, you don't want to know them.

Baldophobes are bimbos. Airheads. The female equivalent of the guy who rates his women friends by the size of their boobs. You want to be judged for what's in your head, not what's on it.

So thanks but no thanks to the scalp refurbishing, Dr. McElwee. I expect you'll have no shortage of customers if and when you do perfect the hair clone thing. Male vanity being the awesome force it is, I wouldn't be surprised to see every dude with a pelt-challenged pate and a credit card lining up at clinics to have their follicles refecundicated, or whatever it is you do.

Every guy except me and Mr. Clean. We'll continue to stand pink and proud.

I may even get myself an earring.

If I'd Known I Was Going to Live This Long . . .

*How long you think that you can run that body
down?*
*How many nights you think that you can do what you
been doing?*

—PAUL SIMON

You know, for a guy who in his time smoked bales of tobacco, swigged oceans of beer and imbibed, ingested or inhaled sundry dubious and occasionally noxious substances ranging from Señor Caliente's Triple X Tabasco Sauce to BC Bud, I've been pretty lucky healthwise. Many friends and colleagues have gone down with wonky knees, blown-out livers and bum tickers, not to mention arthritis, nephritis and bursitis. Me, I keep shuffling along, hunkering just slightly under the Grim Reaper's swathe.

Actually, I think the gods tolerate me. They see me as a source of comic relief. Other folks get cancer, diabetes and galloping brain tumours.

I get bouts of BPPV.

That would stand for Benign Paroxysmal Positional Vertigo. My grandmother would have called them dizzy spells.

It's hardly onerous, as human afflictions go—and you've gotta love any condition that features the word "benign" in its description. My doctor tells me "benign" means it will eventually go away on its own.

The bad news is, it may take twelve weeks.

Having BPPV is like chugalugging two vodka martinis, minus the euphoria. I tend to bump into walls, lurch down staircases and trip over boulders and gopher holes that aren't actually there.

With BPPV, even sitting around the house is a poor man's acid trip. Turn your head suddenly or look up at the ceiling and all sorts of fireworks spontaneously combust behind your eyeballs. The walls undulate. The china cabinet looks like something designed by Gaudí. The floor turns into a downhill slalom course that would give Ken Reid the vapours.

How can you tell whether you've got BPPV or you're just abnormally clumsy? Go to an ear, nose and throat specialist. He or she will sit you in a chair and twist your head hither and yon while peering into your eyes with that pocket high-beam torch they carry.

"What do you see when you look in there?" I ask the ENT guy, my eyes weeping like artesian wells.

"Your eyeball is revolving like a pinwheel," he says.

The culprits that cause BPPV are tiny calcium carbonate crystals in the inner ear. Normally these crystals settle to the bottom of your complicated aural plumbing like tea leaves in the bottom of a cup. With BPPV they shift and drift and brush against microscopic nerve endings. This, in turn confuses the brain and causes the sufferer to behave like Ozzy Osbourne on New Year's Eve.

The cure for BPPV? Assuming you don't want to be crashing into furniture for the next three months, you opt for the Epley Manoeuvre.

That's where Dr. Ear, Nose and Throat plunks you down in a modified dentist's chair, leans you way back and rotates, palpates and generally juggles your noggin until you feel like you've had six vodka martinis plus a ride on the midway Tilt-a-Whirl.

The object is to shake up those crystals of calcium carbonate in your ears in the hopes that they'll settle down where they're supposed to settle down.

The scientific principle here is borrowed from those touristy

Lucite snow globes that you shake up to create a winter scene. The doctor creates a miniblizzard in your skull, then waits for it to subside.

Oh yeah, and one other nifty feature: after you've endured the Epley Manoeuvre, you're instructed not to look up, bend down or lie down for forty-eight hours.

It's one thing to doze in a chair for an hour or so. Sleeping in one for two nights is less thrilling.

Oh well. It leaves you with lots of time to read. And think.

About James Hubert Blake, for instance.

Mr. Blake, better known as Eubie, was a human phenomenon. He smoked cigars, it was said, from the age of six. He played boogie-woogie piano in noisy, dangerous, fume-filled bars for a living. He never drank water.

He died at the age of one hundred.

But not before, in his nineties, he took a long hard look at his life and observed, "If I'd known I was gonna live this long, I'd a taken better care of myself."

When I grow up, I want to be Eubie Blake. Without dizzy spells.

REBOOT

Hello Central, Get Me Nostalgia

I grew up in an Age of Wonders. CCM coaster bikes, Kodak Brownie cameras and gorgeous pine minicabinets that graced the kitchen wall, to name just three. For youngsters in the audience, let me explain how these worked.

The CCM bike had fat, cushiony tires, a spongy, forgiving saddle and one forward gear. The braking system was simple: pedal backwards.

The Kodak Brownie was a square box you could hold in one hand. It had a lens hole at the front, a cranking knob on the side and a shiny black button on the top. To take a photo, you pointed the lens at the subject and pressed the shiny black button. You were done.

The pine minicabinet on the kitchen wall held a charmingly antique Bakelite receiver and an earpiece on a cord. You held the earpiece to your ear and turned a crank on the side. This would summon the dulcet voice of a communications specialist, a lady familiarly known as Central who would briskly and efficiently connect you to whomever in the world you wanted to speak to.

I don't have to tell you where this is going, do I?

Today we ride twenty-four-speed chromium-magnesium alloy Italian racing bikes with toe baskets, hair-trigger handbrakes, Rube Goldbergian derailleurs and saddles that should be cited for sexual interference. The bikes weigh mere grams, cost thousands and crumple like Kleenex at their first encounter with a sewer grate.

And we have digital cameras. Lord, do we have digital cameras. By borrowing against your mortgage, you can become the proud owner of any one of a plethora of sleek, brushed aluminum beauties that make the whole concept of film rolls so yesteryear. Of course you'll need a computer because you'll want to view and sort and crop and enlarge and enhance those photos of cousin Fred wearing the lampshade at your niece's wedding. And a full-colour printer, if you don't already have one.

And miniature! These cameras are so tiny you can slip them in your breast pocket. Although you'll need a wheelbarrow for the instruction manual that tells you how to use them.

And ninety-nine percent of us use these marvels for the same purpose our grandparents used the Kodak Brownie—to take mediocre pictures with which to bore our relatives.

Telephones? Those elegant wooden wall *objets d'art* have been reduced to bland plastic wafers that follow and bedevil us everywhere we go. As for convenience, here's what I have to do to reach Aunt Edna in Red Deer. Pick up phone. Open phone. Punch in my calling card number (eleven digits). Listen to Robotress welcome me to the phone service for which I shell out fifty bucks a month, then respond to prompts. *For service in English* (punch) . . . *to place a long distance call* (punch) . . . *To charge this call to a calling card, enter* . . . (punchpunchpunchpunchpunchpunchpunchpunch) . . . *Please enter the number you are calling* . . . Another ten digits.

Back in the good old days, you just cranked up the nice lady at Central. She did all the heavy lifting.

My point—and there is one—is not that we should go back to the days of party lines and Kodak Brownies and CCM one-speeds . . . but could we just tap the coaster brakes a little? Look! The Gillette Company has just introduced its latest contender in the men's shaving sweepstakes—a safety razor with *five* blades.

Five blades! To shave whiskers off a chin!

We're overtechnologized, folks. It's getting silly.

Fortunately I'm not the only one who's noticed. Boffins at the telecommunications giant NTT DoCoMo are bringing out a brand new cell phone with revolutionary features. You want a phone that you can take photos with? Or download clips from the latest Bruce Willis flick? Or play Texas hold'em, send emails, check the stock market or google your family tree back eleven generations?

Then this phone is not for you. What you can do with this phone is make and receive telephone calls.

That's it. And because it lacks the extra features, this phone—its nickname is Elderphone, guess why—boasts fewer confusing buttons and a bigger keypad with larger type that you can actually see without getting out your reading glasses. Plus the battery lasts five times longer, because it doesn't have to work so hard.

Allen Nogee, a communications analyst, observes, "There is still a very large number of users who only talk [on the phone] and are frustrated by all the other features."

To which this elder can only say, "Well, duh."

And also hooray. It ain't "Hello Central, get me Aunt Edna," but it's a start.

No Spam, Thank You, Ma'am

Just a few short years ago it was a not-terribly-chic luncheon meat. Or at best a song from a Monty Python skit.

Today it is a global migraine. A multigazillion-dollar ripoff scam and a mammoth pain in the inbox for computer users everywhere.

I speak, but of course, of spam.

In case you've been living under a laundry hamper for the past dozen or so years, let me explain: spam is junk email. The blackfly of online activity. Mass blitzkrieg advertising of crap that nobody asked for and nobody wants but everybody finds in their You've Got Mail slot virtually every time they fire up their desktop or laptop.

Why does spam advertising work? For the same reason that fishing with hand grenades works. You lob enough explosives into the lake and something will float to the surface. Similarly, if you blanket email several hundred thousand unsuspecting recipients, a profitable few will be stupid enough to respond, no matter how moronic the pitch.

Just how dumb can people be? Hey. Who's President of the United States?

There are ways to combat spammers. The internet abounds with antispam software—much of it free—which will intercept the spam-spewing swine and deflect their unwanted missives into deepest cyberspace.

But spammers, alas, are endlessly creative. Close one rathole and they gnaw themselves another. I, for instance, am well protected from online spammers.

But now the beggars are coming through my fax machine.

One in particular. It calls itself The Travel Center and it offers me, at least three times a week, "fantastic bargains" on cruises to "Orlando, Ft. Lauderdale and Bahamas."

I do not wish to cruise to any of the above-mentioned destinations. Even if I did, I certainly would not do it through a company that besieges me with unasked-for come-ons and uses up my fax paper.

Happily there is a number at the bottom of their advertisement that you can call to be removed from their advertising list. I called that number.

Ten times. The faxes kept coming.

So I phoned the main number (the one you call to sign up for a cruise).

Five times. Each time an operator assured me that I was off the list and the faxes would cease.

They didn't. I called a sixth time and told the woman who answered that I would never book with them because I had asked very politely fifteen times to *please stop the faxes.* She hung up on me.

So I called the Canadian Radio and Television Commission in Ottawa. They told me that since it was an American travel company, I should call the Federal Communications Commission in Washington. The FCC operator told me my complaint would be filed and the travel company would be "dealt with."

That was three weeks ago. While waiting for the FCC to act, I have received eleven faxes from the travel company.

It's too bad the Travel Center is located in Florida and not Russia. They know how to handle spammers in Russia—ask Vardan Kushnir.

Oh sorry, you can't. Mr. Kushnir is dead. Bludgeoned to death in his Moscow apartment by persons unknown. Do the police have any suspects? Yes, several million. Vardan Kushnir was Russia's most notorious spammer, believed to have clogged the inbox of nearly every Russian who had an email account. Kushnir was killed after someone posted his home address on the web, and Russian newspapers reacted with undisguised glee. "The Spammer Had It Coming," read one headline. And another, "An Ultimate Solution to the Spam Problem."

I wouldn't want to see anything that gruesome happen to spammers in this part of the world, but I wouldn't object if our research labs started using spammers in place of laboratory rats.

It's a natural when you think about it. Research scientists sometimes get too attached to laboratory rats. That wouldn't happen with spammers. PETA would have no objections if animal experimentation was conducted exclusively on spammers.

Besides. There are certain things a rat just won't do.

If the Shoe Fits, Shuck It

Our life is frittered away by detail . . . Simplify,
simplify, simplify!

—Henry David Thoreau

The Walden Pond wise man found the nineteenth century too complicated? I wonder what he'd make of Planet Earth if he was around today. *Maclean's* magazine for example. I'm sitting here looking at a full-page IBM ad in *Maclean's* that consists of six paragraphs of ad copy. Here's one of them: "DB2 takes full advantage of your existing heterogeneous and open environments, while its leading-edge autonomic computing technology means increased reliability, increased programmer productivity and decreased deployment and management costs."

IBM forked over thousands of dollars to put that ad before my eyes, and I have no idea what in hell they're trying to sell me.

But why pick on IBM? An army of merchandisers out there flogs merchandise that's straight from Neptune. There's a refrigerator—strike that—a "food management system" on the market that comes with a video camera (to leave messages for the kids), an electronic calendar (to remind me when Lent rolls around) and an on-board computer where I can store three hundred recipes.

Will it keep my beer cold? The ads don't say.

And simple sunglasses? They've been rendered hopelessly

obsolete by "digital eyewear." Oakley's is marketing a three-hundred-dollar set of shades called Thump. Oakley Thumps feature (I'm quoting here from another all-but-indecipherable ad) "an integrated music player with nonexpandable 512 MB of memory." Near as I can figure, this means that Thumps have a built-in hi-fi that sits on your left temple feeding favourite ditties into your ear.

Presumably Thumps will also keep the sun out of your eyes.

And then there's the running shoe. There was a time when running shoes were pretty basic—a slab of moulded rubber with a canvas upper that attached to your feet by means of two long strings. Lace 'em up and off you trot.

Not any more. Now we have basketball shoes (high-rise uppers to protect the ankles) and aerobics shoes (extra-light to fight "foot fatigue"). We have skateboarding shoes (thin soles so you can feel the board) and cheerleading shoes (notches for your fingers to grab during stunts). Looking for a sole with more soul? Reebok offers the ZanChi Yoga/Pilates shoes. To help you "find your inner 'chi.'"

We even have, God help us, a specific footwear niche for "walking" shoes.

To help you, you know, walk.

And then there's the all-new Adidas_1. The world's first "intelligent shoe." Adidas_1 shoes contain a microprocessor more powerful than the first Mac computer. It "reads" the road as you run. A magnetic sensor in the heel decides whether the terrain is too soft or too hard and then, by means of a teensy built-in motor, adjusts the cushioning accordingly. The Adidas_1 retails at a shop near me for three hundred dollars plus. Intelligent? At that price it had better be able to fill out my income tax form.

If, like me, you find these tootsie options a tad pricey and confusing, there is a cheaper alternative. You could go barefoot.

The latest trend, folks. Many professional sprinters are opting to run and jog wearing no shoes at all. Why not? Zola Budd was a world-class runner who won the international cross-country championship twice without shoes. Ethiopian marathoner Abebe Bikila ran barefoot at the Rome Olympics in 1960—and took home the gold medal. A growing number of participants regularly complete the Boston Marathon, all twenty-six miles, 385 yards of it, running *sans* shoes.

There's even a school of thought that believes running shoes might be *bad* for the feet—that they pamper and coddle muscles and tendons that would be strengthened if the owner trained *au naturel*. Ben Kotanen operates a store for runners in Surrey, BC, but on his own time he trains in bare feet. "The foot is well-designed," he says. "If you run in proper form, you don't need the cushioning."

Running without specialized, hi-tech, overpriced shoes? The athletic footwear industry sells fifteen billion dollars' worth of fancy foot gear to North Americans every year. Are they going to let this new trend walk all over them?

Of course not. Nike has already responded with its newest product, the Nike Free. This shoe comes with ultralight uppers, maximum flexibility and almost no sole at all to give the wearer the exact sensations one would experience if one was . . . shoeless.

So now they want to sell me shoes so minimal it's like wearing no shoes at all?

I don't know about the rest of the Emperor's clothes, but I'm pretty sure he's buck naked from the ankles down.

Me and Mustang Sally

So I'm in an airport far from home, standing at the rent-a-car counter, ready to pick up my prearranged two-door, midsize, no-name, probably grey, who-cares sedan. I'm familiar with the drill. I cough up my driver's licence, credit card, name, address and phone number—just as I've done umpteen dozen times before.

Except this time the clerk looks up, winks, and says, "How about a Mustang?"

"Say what?" I reply cleverly.

"A Mustang GT," says the clerk out of the side of his mouth. "Candy-apple red. Goes like a bat outta Hades."

I'm pretty sure he winked again.

The suggestion is, of course, patently absurd. The Mustang automobile is a vehicle pretty much reserved for young, lithe, testosterone-charged studs. I am a rickety dotard, bald of pate and grey of beard, who normally drives a beige Subaru station wagon. I have absolutely no business attempting to wedge my portly carcass behind the wheel of a candy-apple red Mustang.

"I'll take it," I say.

And why not? Over the years on various business trips and sundry vacations, I've commandeered the ignition keys of a parking lot's worth of Avis, Hertz, and Budget buggies. The cars I've rented have invariably been sensible, economical, no-nonsense . . .

And utterly forgettable. I can't remember a single make or model.

So why not—just once—a candy-apple red Mustang GT?

And she's a beauty. I find her nestled in stall A-7, crouched like a hungry panther, ready to spring out and take down a wildebeest. I pop the trunk, heave in my luggage, swagger to the driver's door and swing it open casually, the way I imagine Johnny Depp might do it. His Dudeness is ready to roll.

Except the car is . . . incredibly low. Somehow I can't quite get my knees high enough or my butt low enough to actually, you know, *get into* the driver's seat. I think I hear muffled snickers from the depths of the airport parking garage.

The snickers are but the first of many humiliations I will encounter driving the car I still think of semiaffectionately as Mustang Sally.

For one thing, ignition. When I turn the key (having finally corkscrewed my body into the minuscule bucket behind the steering wheel), I am rewarded with a roar that sounds like a Saturn rocket at launch. I actually jump. Palms sweating, I put the car into drive and tentatively feather the gas pedal. Mustang Sally lunges forth like a slingshot dragster. I proceed through the airport parking lot in a series of squealing, rubber-burning lurches, desperately riding the gas and the brake pedals with either foot.

It doesn't get better out on the street. At the first stoplight, a mullet-headed goon driving a Trans Am pulls up beside me, looks over, guns his engine and smirks. I pretend to be searching for CBC-FM on my dashboard radio. He's waiting for me at the second stop-light. And the third. At the fourth stoplight he's beside me again, still smirking, still revving. I check the horizon for prowling police cars and see none. When the light goes green I mutter, "Oh hell," and mash the gas pedal to the floor.

I cover the next hundred metres staring goggle-eyed at my own overhead dome light, my neck cranked back in classic whiplash for-mation. Even though the Trans Am has disappeared, I chalk it up as a win. After all, I didn't hit anything.

I drove Mustang Sally for the next six days. According to the ads, I should have been a man transformed. The experience ought to have turned me into a younger, leaner, edgier studmuffin.

Mostly just a muffin. Mustang Sally rear-ended my composure and left big, black tread marks all over my self-respect. I can't count the number of times I embarrassed myself trying to fake Guy Car Talk with other drivers eager to chat about RPMs, compression ratios, bore and stroke and other automotive unfathomables.

"Slick rig, man. How many cubic inches?"

"Gee, I dunno. Fifty, maybe?"

And I'll never forget the mortification of driving past young women. Each time their lovely heads would swivel towards me at the sound of Sally's throaty rumble. Each time their bright eyes would sparkle expectantly at the sight of Sally's sleek red flanks sliding into view.

Each time their sweet red mouths would morph into an "Eeww" when they beheld the geezer at the wheel.

Still, I survived. I got Mustang Sally back to her rent-a-car corral at the airport with nary a dent, scratch or speeding ticket. When I went inside to settle up, the same clerk was at the counter.

"So howdja like the Mustang?" he asked.

I'm pretty sure he winked again.

Potholes are Good for Us

What defines life on the Gulf Islands? Well, if you asked a half-dozen Gulf Islanders you'd probably get at least six different answers. Among them: serenity, lush scenery, laid-back lifestyle—not to mention dependence on BC Ferries and the privilege of paying ten cents a litre more for gas than you do on the mainland. But none of those are the true defining characteristic of living in the Gulf Islands, no. What really sets us apart from the rest of the world is our potholes.

Man, have we got potholes. Oh, the main roads are pretty good, but point your hood ornament down some of our secondary roads and you are in for a ride that makes whitewater rafting look like a paddle in the kiddies' pool.

And I'm not talking about temporary, pop-up-in-midwinter, paved-over-by-late-spring potholes here. In the Gulf Islands we have *heritage* potholes. Entire generations have grown up dodging the same roadway caverns, canyons and crevasses. Some of our potholes are so old they have First Nations names.

I could never understand why our potholes endured so long until a letter to the editor of our local paper, the *Driftwood,* explained it all. It's because our potholes are good for us. The letter was written by Jean Gelwicks, a well-known environmentalist and avid cyclist. In essence her letter said, don't think of our potholes as potholes, think of them as complimentary speed bumps.

Perhaps, her letter suggests, the condition of our roads forces us to go more slowly.

"Maybe," she writes, "the potholes say that islanders are not so driven by the automobile as people in the city. Maybe they say we don't even care if we have to travel slowly. In fact, maybe we like going slowly . . . We can enjoy the views of our hedgerows, pastures, trees, glimpses of the ocean and maybe a deer or two as we drive slowly down our roads."

Well sure. Makes sense. Only a fool (or a first-time tourist) drives fast on island secondary roads. It could cost you your entire undercarriage.

Jean Gelwicks' letter reminded me of a place I used to live in rural Ontario. The secondary road that ran by my front gate featured a beautiful old railway underpass built in the late 1800s out of huge blocks of hand-hewn limestone. In its heyday, I suppose, the trains went over and the buggies and Model Ts went under. That bridge was beautiful, and now that I think of it, it was kind of our community speed bump. The bridge was built to accommodate horse-drawn wagons and Model Ts. Not SUVs and cube vans and Hummers. You had to drive really slowly and negotiate the underpass one vehicle at a time. More than one driver in a hurry left streaks of fender paint on those limestone blocks.

Alas, the trains disappeared and the tracks were torn up, but the bridge remained, slowing down vehicular traffic in both directions. So naturally the town fathers voted to demolish the bridge.

They called it a bottleneck. They tore it down and paved the road and widened it so that within a year the road was handling eighty percent more traffic including dump trucks and tractor-trailers that used it as a shortcut to the highway. Brave New World.

Recently I spent a few weeks in the south of Spain, where the approaches to many small Andalucian towns feature what they call a *policía dormido*—a sleeping policeman. It's a ridge of concrete (frequently unmarked) that runs right across the road. Hit it at thirty kilometres an hour or less and you'll notice a bump, but you'll be okay. Hit it at highway speeds and you'll be airborne. Savvy Spaniards tend not to speed through those small towns.

All comes down to how you look at the world. I see down in the States that the US Chamber of Commerce is going after hybrid cars. They're asking Congress to impose a special tax on the hybrids because, the Chamber of Commerce spokesman complained, "those cars consume less fuel than regular cars and therefore aren't paying their share of the gasoline tax."

Potholes or speed bumps? Depends on your point of view.

As Jean Gelwicks says in her letter, "Perhaps our pothole-riddled roads remind us of a time when everyone travelled more slowly. When there were fewer cars on the road and people walked more."

Could be. And maybe they serve to remind us that driving down the road is as good a time as any to slow down. Roll down the window, smell the Nootka roses. And take in the Big Picture.

A Cyberfridge? Thanks
But No Thanks

M r. Frank Lee
Marketing Manager
LG Electronics Canada, Ltd.

Dear Frank,

Caught a magazine review of your company's all new, state-of-the-art Internet Refrigerator recently. Wow! Have I got this right? A refrigerator with a built-in computer that can hold a database of three hundred recipes? And it'll inform me of which ingredients I don't have on hand? And I can then order the missing ingredients? From an online grocer? All without even leaving my fridge?

I also understand that I no longer have to worry about festering green furry mystery foodstuffs lurking at the back of the shelf. The LG Internet Refrigerator monitors the expiry date of everything on the shelves and reminds me which foods to eat before they go bad.

It says in the magazine article that your Internet Refrigerator's got a built-in camera so that I can leave video messages for the kids.

140

And a built-in electronic calendar to alert me to "food events" like Lent, the weekly meat draw at the Legion and which day my vegetarian cousin is coming for dinner.

This is some machine, Frank, a refrigerator with a built-in television with satellite access. Not to mention an MP3 player with surround-sound stereo speakers. I haven't even mentioned the tastefully inlaid colour touchscreen so that I can surf the net or play online blackjack while I'm waiting for my coffee to . . . download, I guess.

You're quoted in this article, Frank. It says, "Frank Lee, marketing manager for LG Electronics Canada Inc., says the LG Internet Refrigerator is more than a mere food-management system. He calls it 'a communications centre.'"

Know what I call it, Frank? I call it the worst idea since the behind-the-back three-hook bra fastener.

At any rate, Frank, I'm way ahead of you. My refrigerator already *is* a communications system.

But let's take it from the inside out. I figure that my fridge (six-year-old Maytag, $675.00) performs as well internally as your brand-new hi-tech job (eleven thousand—are you serious—eleven thousand nine hundred and ninety-nine dollars?). Both units keep the butter firm, the lettuce crisp and the houseflies out. But it's the outside of my fridge that kicks butt, communications-wise. Check it out, Frank. Thanks to the miracle of fridge magnets, you can see a photo of my brother straddling his prized candy-apple red Kawasaki Drifter. You can see my sister with her six kids and nineteen grandkids all lined up and grinning in front of a stone wall in Rockwood, Ontario. There's a glossy print of the giant Russian sunflowers we grew in our garden last summer—five metres high with blossoms the size of hubcaps. I've got snaps from the Fall Fair and the big snowfall last January. And an X-rated one of Wally dropping his drawers to show off his patriotic red gotchies at last year's Canada Day celebration. Here's one of Lynne and me wearing hats made out of an inner tube and beach flotsam at that crazy karaoke party in Mexico last winter.

Communications system? I've got my whole *life* stuck to my fridge, Frank.

There's hard copy too—like the grocery list for Tuesday and a

Xerox of my niece Ruby's report card. I see a bill marked "overdue" from my friendly telephone company. And check out that drawing by the door handle, a nativity scene rendered on a serviette with a full palette of Crayola markers, a masterpiece crafted last Christmas by Owen, a visiting six-year-old.

I'm pretty sure it's a nativity scene.

The point I'm trying to make here, Frank, is: Thanks but no thanks. I wouldn't have your Brave New Fridge in my kitchen as a gift. Why? Well, for one thing I don't want a refrigerator that's smarter than me.

Number two, I'm not keen on owning a storage system in which I have to "enter" the contents twice, once physically and then again via a keyboard.

Number three: I'm just an old-fashioned guy at heart, Frank. Why would I want a refrigerator with a brain?

I've got one with soul.

Slow Down, You Move Too Fast

A different kind of political campaign is a-building on the Gulf Islands. This one's not going to involve garish Day-Glo "vote for me" signs pasted on trees and pounded into lawns. There will be no snide and snarky radio attack ads or venomous TV spots. No hopeful candidates with sheaves of brochures tucked under their arms will besmirch our yards or knock on the door right in the middle of Paul Kennedy and *Ideas*.

This campaign will be the antithesis—the mirror opposite—of that frenetic, splenetic barnstorming fireball our politicians regularly put us through.

If I had to sum up this new campaign in one breath, I'd use a line from an old Simon and Garfunkel song. The line that goes, "Slow down, you move too fast."

We do, you know—move too fast, I mean. And we're moving faster all the time. Just in the past ten or fifteen years, laptops, cell phones and BlackBerrys have practically become part of the mandatory dress code. And food. What's faster than food these days? Crave your morning breakfast, but can't spare the time to actually sit down at a table and eat it? Breakaway Foods developed just the product line for you. They called it IncrEdibles. Think of all your favourite morning treats—scrambled eggs, macaroni and cheese, pancakes with syrup . . .

On a stick. Like a Popsicle. Perfect. You could eat it at the wheel while you waited for the light to change.

It's crazy, folks. It couldn't last. Something had to give. And it has. At least where I live. It's called the Slow Islands campaign.

And that's pretty much it, campaign-wise. Just go slower. How? Well, how about hopping on the bike instead of firing up the car for that five-minute trip to the supermarket? Better still, how about forgetting the supermarket? How about cycling up that farm lane on the way to town? The one with the sign that reads "Farm Fresh Eggs" and "Veggies in Season."

Slow down. Find out what really fresh food tastes like.

Want to decelerate even more? Plant some veggie seeds in your back yard. Watch your own garden grow. Find out what really *really* fresh food tastes like.

Lots of ways you can join the Slow Island movement—even if you're off-island. Don't have time, you say? Well, take it back. It's yours. It was stolen from you. We don't have to blow up the TV as John Prine advocates, but we can turn it off. Read a book. Watch a sunset. Pat the dog.

I don't know how this works into Einstein's Theory of Relativity, but I'm finding that when I go slower, I actually *gain* time.

When I drive into town these days, I drive below the speed limit. If somebody comes up behind me, I just pull over and let them pass. Takes me a few minutes longer to get to town, but I actually enjoy the trip.

And I gave up my gas lawn mower this year. Bought one of those antediluvian push mowers instead. I used to spend about half an hour inhaling exhaust fumes, courting a migraine from the noise and wondering if I could drive to town before I bled to death in the event I lawn-mowered my foot off.

Now I spend about twice as long cutting the lawn with my push mower, but it's quality time. I get a modest workout. And the rhythmic fluttering of the lawn mower isn't loud enough to drown out the robins and the blackbirds.

You want to join the Slow Islands movement? Okay. You're in. No membership dues, no meetings, no waivers to sign or pledges to honour. Just . . . slow down.

We don't have T-shirts or lapel pins, either, but it's not hard to recognize your fellow members.

We're always relaxed. We're usually smiling. And we're going as slow as we want.

Seemed Like a Good Idea
at the Time

An idea isn't responsible for the people who believe in it.

—Don Marquis

Sometimes I've believed as many as six impossible things before breakfast.

—Lewis Carroll

The older I get, the more I realize that most of life is really quite black and white. Except when it's off-white. Or pearl grey. Or ivory, charcoal, ecru, ebony or milky.

The truth is, the older I get, the more I realize that everything I thought was rock solid and untransmutable ain't necessarily so.

Take water. The very essence of life, right? Can't get enough water. That's why you see young trendies lugging around plastic bottles of Evian and Dasani as if they were fixing to cross the Kalahari, even when they're only going shopping at the mall. Stands to reason. Experts have been telling us for years that we need to drink seven tall glasses of water every day. Or is it twelve?

According to a recent American medical study, the correct answer is less—a *lot* less. In fact, according to Dr. Marvin Adner who headed up the study, we're all drinking way too much water—especially the healthy athletic types among us. The study looked at nearly five hundred marathon runners and discovered that many of them are downing so much water they are diluting their blood—with potentially fatal results. Gulping too much water can cause a condition called hyponatremia—critically low blood-sodium levels. If the levels get too low, it means brain damage and eventually death.

Then there's the sun. Ever since human bungling led to holes in the ozone layer, experts have been warning us about UV indexes and the importance of slathering great gobs of sunblock all over our carcasses before we venture outdoors.

Well, not all experts. Some of them are now arguing that we need *more* unscreened sunlight in our lives. Dr. Michael Holick of the Boston University Medical Center has published a book extolling the virtues of unprotected sunbathing. He argues that it boosts levels of vitamin D in the skin. Orthodox dermatologists are predictably outraged, but an organization called The Vitamin D Council backs Dr. Holick, saying it's time to rethink our solar attitudes.

Who ya gonna believe?

And Mr. Hughes, if you're reading this, I want you to know that you were wrong too. Mr. Hughes was my grade five teacher. He lurked over me and my classmates for one entire horrible school year and once fetched me a crack across the knuckles with his ruler just because I dozed off for a few seconds during one of his interminable droning lectures.

Naps are *good* things, you pontificating sadist! In fact, *you'd* have been better off catching a few winks instead of terrorizing your charges. According to a study published in the American Geriatrics Society Journal, people—older adults particularly—are mentally sharper if they nod off for an hour or so in the early afternoon.

Spaniards with their siestas figured this out about five hundred years ago, but North Americans are slow learners.

And now it seems that computers, commonly touted as the greatest human innovation since fire, the wheel and the dashboard coffee cup holder, may in fact be hazardous to our health. Particularly if you're a male laptop user. Turns out that laptops are hazardous to our, er, laps.

Genital scorching is what we're talking about, men. *Lancet,* the British medical journal, has reported a case in which a laptop-tapping patient suffered burns to his penis and scrotum, apparently caused by the machine in his lap. Scientists did some research and found that as portable machines go, laptop computers are indeed hot potatoes, often generating surface temperatures in excess of forty degrees Celsius. Add to that the internal body temperature generated by squeezing your thighs together to hold the laptop steady— and that makes it mighty toasty for The Boys.

Dangerously toasty? Could be. Scientists say that a temperature increase of just one degree Celsius in the scrotum can reduce sperm production by forty percent.

Dr. Marc Goldstein, a fertility expert at Cornell University says, "It makes perfect sense, but no one had thought about the fertility effect of a hot computer on your lap."

So let's sum up. Laptops: bad. Naps: good. Water: bad. Sunshine: good.

Can't wait 'til someone comes out with a study showing that eating grease, chugalugging rum and chain-smoking Marlboros makes you smarter and better-looking. It's only a matter of time.

Got a Problem?
Use Your Head

*I like a man who likes to see a fine barn as well as a
good tragedy.*

—RALPH WALDO EMERSON

Drew Garland was one of those problem students. Class dis-
rupter. Mouthy to his teachers. Surly, lazy and unmotivated. It
finally came to a head when the seventeen-year-old got into a beef
on the school bus. The driver had had it with the spitballs and the
potty mouth and the brawling with other riders. Drew Garland was
kicked off the bus and barred from riding it for the rest of the school
year.

Driving himself to school was not an option and neither was
quitting, so Drew did the only thing he could. He started hoofing
the four kilometres to and from class.

It changed his life. Because a bad attitude was not Drew
Garland's big problem. His big problem was that he was . . . big. A
hundred and fifty-four kilos big. His daily eight-kilometre "workout" helped him drop forty-five kilos of couch-potato baby fat and
nudged him out of his sedentary, mind-fermenting lifestyle.

Simple solutions—sometimes they're right in front of our faces.

The folks in Derrinallum, Australia, know all about that. The town cemetery was approaching corpse capacity with nowhere to expand, but Aussies are not the kind of folks to take a problem like that lying down. So very soon Derrinallumites who reach their expiry date will be buried, not in a traditional coffin stretched out in a plot of earth of three cubic metres, but in simple biodegradable body bags.

Standing up.

Like a fence post—only two metres under.

Why not? It saves space, goes easier on the environment and—hey, do you care if you're planted horizontally or vertically? Only the gophers will know.

There are practical solutions all around us to most of life's problems, had we but the wit to recognize them. Did you know that Coca Cola is excellent for scrubbing off the crud that collects on battery terminals? That the Avon bath oil Skin So Soft is like Agent Orange to mosquitoes and black flies? That one's sex life can be enhanced by chewing Altoids? (Hint: Monica Lewinsky was a big Altoids fan.)

Examples everywhere. Take clotheslines.

I know, I know. You seldom see a working clothesline any more, and that's a pity. Clotheslines are one of the best energy savers that human ingenuity ever came up with.

I remember my mother's clotheslines. She had three of them, and she worked them briskly just about every sunny day we got. I can still see my dad's long johns billowing like spinnakers, hear the chalk-on-blackboard scrawk of the pulleys and smell the outside freshness of my line-dried pillowcase as I buried my face in it.

The monotone howl of the basement spin dryer isn't quite in the same league.

Clotheslines are classically simple—and big money savers to boot. Experts say the average family can save about a thousand kilowatt hours annually, even if they only use the clothesline nine months out of the year.

Well, some experts say that. Others say, "Sorry, ma'am, but that clothesline is against the law. You have forty-eight hours to take it down or face prosecution."

It's true. Outdoor clotheslines are illegal in many jurisdictions in the USA and Canada. Why? Aesthetics. Some brain-dead function-ary somewhere decided that clothes drying on a line detract from the clean uncluttered sightlines of suburban cupcake architecture. The idea was viral. Today in parts of California, they have clothes-line patrol units that prowl select neighbourhoods in search of ver-boten laundry flapping in the breeze.

Which goes to prove that just because an idea's practical doesn't mean we're savvy enough to grasp it.

But I have faith. And I think now that we're all facing the strato-spheric oil prices the rest of the world has to put up with, we're going to get a lot smarter fast. Clotheslines will be chic. Our garage doors will grow cobwebs as we all get out and walk to the corner store, swathed in Skin So Soft to keep the bugs at bay.

It's all very simple, really.

As Monica might say, just use your head.

Snoozing is Good for You

So I'm humping through Vancouver's International Airport, already jet-lagged and frantically searching for Gate 47A so I can catch flight 8960B, which I'm pretty sure—if I can decipher the drone on the public address system—is in the final stages of boarding. I round a corner and behold, three snow-white sarcophagi splayed out on the terrazzo. They look like something out of *Star Trek*. Large cylindrical pods with what looks like a single bed jutting out of one side, each pod big enough to engulf a human body. Indeed, one of them has the better part of a man's pair of trousered legs sticking out of it.

"What the hell is that?" I ask.

"That's a MetroNaps EnergyPod," the smiling attendant explains, handing me a brochure. I read the fine print. For a mere fifteen dollars, I can buy twenty uninterrupted minutes to recline in one of these gizmos, wherein an assortment of vibrations and "sounds from nature" will block out the hustle-bustle and hurly-burly of the world around me, allowing me a microsnooze.

A quick nap in the middle of a crisis-heavy day, smack in the centre of a busy airport. Sounds daft, but some experts say it's an idea that's overdue. Experts like Bob Stickgold, assistant professor of psychiatry at Harvard Medical School. Stickgold says that all of us need more sleep than we're getting. He warns, in fact, that an appalling percentage of us are little more than walking zombies. Our banzai lifestyle is leaving us seriously sleep-deprived, and that's not good for us—or for the people around us.

"You're phenomenally stupid when you're sleep-deprived, and you're too stupid to realize it," says Stickgold. "We [humans] are the only known organism that sleep-deprives itself."

And it costs us big. The *Exxon Valdez* oil spill was blamed on a captain who was groggy from too much booze and too little sleep. The Chernobyl nuclear disaster was caused by overworked and under-rested reactor personnel. We'll never know how many plane crashes, train wrecks and highway collisions could be chalked up to simple human fatigue.

It seems like a cruel joke. Our ancestors would have killed for the labour-saving devices that we take for granted. But the irony is that our ancestors, overworked as they were, got way more sleep than we do. They napped regularly, and by and large, they went to bed and got up with the sun. They didn't have alarm clocks to jangle them awake in the predawn murk or electric lights to keep them up after dusk. They didn't punch time clocks or pack BlackBerrys on their hips, and they didn't mainline coffee for a chemical buzz to get them through the nine-to-five.

Which is another thing our ancestors didn't have—a nine-to-five template to fit their working hours into. That's a regime that works well for factories and offices, but not so well for the average human body.

We all have biological clocks, and they operate in a completely different time zone. Left to our own devices, without artificial stimulants like fluorescent lights, looming deadlines and a baleful boss staring meaningfully at the office clock, most of us would probably fall asleep between one and four in the morning and one in four in the afternoon. That's when our eyelids naturally get heavy, our body temperature drops significantly and our Inner Cro-Magnon subconsciously starts looking for a cozy cave and a nice sabretooth tiger skin rug to curl up in.

But we're not allowed to. It's against the rules. So we suck back another espresso, rub our eyes, go back to the grind and make one more deposit in our sleep deprivation account.

That goes a long way to explaining the presence of those power-nap chair pods I saw in the Vancouver airport—which I've learned are destined to show up eventually in shopping malls, office lobbies, train stations, bus depots and anywhere else frazzled folks might be tempted to buy a little peace and quiet.

So did I go for it? Did I spend fifteen bucks for twenty minutes of intense napping?

Are you kidding—and miss my flight?

Besides, I had an ace in the hole and I knew it.

I was heading for Mexico. Land of the siesta.

Measure for Measure

*It has been over 30 years since we were first
introduced to the metre, litre, kilogram, and Celsius.
It is not an exaggeration to say that we are now all
familiar with metric. Nearly 10-million Canadians
have learned metric in public school since the mid-
1970s while the rest have learned metric from the
media, marketplace, and government.*

That's a quote from *One Metre,* an online propaganda service bill-
ing itself as "Canada's Metric Website since 1998." Only the first
sentence is accurate—Ottawa did formally announce that Canada
was going metric back in 1970.

The rest of the quote is wishful thinking. Canadians—the ones
I meet and deal with anyway—have neither converted to metric nor
rushed to embrace it. Thirty-five years on, we still buy our house
paint in gallons, set our ovens in Fahrenheit, frame our houses with
two-by-fours and wash down our quarter-pounders with a pint or
two of beer.

The metric system is not unknown to us. We see kilometres on
our highway signs and we hear millimetres and degrees Celsius in
Environment Canada forecasts. Metric—by government mandate—
is in our lives, but not our hearts. I don't know a soul who gives his
height in centimetres or her weight in kilograms—do you?

After three and a half decades of dedicated indoctrination by Canada's ever-compliant media, I still have no clear idea of the size of a hectare, what a kilopascal represents or even how to pronounce "tonne."

This shotgun marriage isn't working.

It's on the rocks in Britain, too, and they've been bickering about metric since 1965. The British government is even more jackbootish about metric conversion than Ottawa. By 2009 British shopkeepers will be forbidden—that's right, forbidden—to use the word "pound" or "foot" in any sale.

Brave New World, anyone?

Fans of metrification point out the impracticality of the imperial system. They are absolutely right. It is impractical. Gloriously so—just like the language we all share. The English-speaking world has bumbled along with imperial measurements since the thirteenth century, when King Edward I decreed that a common yardstick be used throughout his kingdom. And how long would this "yard" be? Simple—the distance from King Eddie's royal schnozz to the tip of his outstretched fingers.

Compared with metric, that's downright primitive. The "metre" is exactly one ten-millionth of the distance from the equator to the North Pole.

A little tough to pace off, but accurate to a fault.

Give metric its due: it is impeccably precise and scientific. Great for sending rockets to Saturn but woefully mundane for normal discourse. "Five-foot-two, eyes of blue," works nicely as a song lyric. "One hundred and fifty-seven-point-five-eight centimetres, eyes of blue" does not.

Besides, we *can't* get rid of the old system—not as long as our biggest trading partner (you know who I mean) shows diddly-squat interest in converting to metric. We're going to need our pounds and ounces, feet and inches for the foreseeable future.

So should we just chuck out metric and revert to imperial? Nah, that won't happen—nor should it. The radical proposal I'm making is, let's have both. Officially, I mean.

Why not? This is an adaptable, resilient country. Canuck Anglophones weathered the trauma of seeing French on corn flakes boxes at the breakfast table. We could easily juggle two systems of measurement. That way the bean-counters and anal retentives could have their metric, and old-fart romantics like me could hang on to our fathoms and furlongs, bushels and pecks.

But it's not just about nostalgia, it's also about useful information. I recently heard a CBC radio host blurt that we'd received "an inch and a half" of rain over the weekend. Nowadays that's probably a firing offence at the CBC, but I could have kissed her. I can *visualize* an inch and a half of rain. It speaks to me in a way that "thirty-nine millimetres" never will. I long to hear my radio tell me it's "ninety-five in the shade" in Hamilton, or that St. John's is nestled under "two feet of snow."

It's more personal than that. If I hear the cops are looking for a serial killer of bald writers, and he's 187 centimetres tall and weighs ninety-one kilograms, I don't know whether to be on the lookout for a guy who's long and lean or short and dumpy. Mutt or Jeff? Laurel or Hardy? If the APB says the guy is six-foot-two, two hundred pounds, I know exactly what to look for. A police station to hide in.

C'mon Ottawa—cut us some slack. Give us an inch on this. We won't take a kilometre.

Keep It Simple, Sony

*Once the WLT signal was received all the way to the
Alleghenies and west to the Rockies, but that was
when radio amounted to something and radios were
built to pull in signals. The Zenith had a tuning knob
as big as a grapefruit. You'd spin that and bring in
Nashville and Cincinnati and Detroit and Little Rock
and Salt Lake City, but the plastic pisspot radios you
bought nowadays wouldn't get a signal from thirty
miles away.*

—Garrison Keillor

Ah, knobs like grapefruits. I remember them well. Back in my
teens we had a twenty-one inch, black-and-white Admiral TV
that featured just two knobs, both of hockey puck if not grapefruit
proportions. One knob turned the TV off and on and controlled the
volume; the other was numbered one to twelve, just like a clock. Our
television universe was a dozen channels, several frequently "off the
air" and featuring what looked like extreme close-ups of blizzards.
If you clicked through one to twelve and found nothing of interest,
your evening of television was done, and you went looking for a
book.

The TV in my house right now gets ... I don't know, a hundred?

three hundred? channels, and it doesn't matter because I seldom watch any of them. I watch less TV today then I did in 1956.

I can't. It's too hard to turn on my television.

The knob like a grapefruit is long gone. I have teensy chrome buttons the size of fingernail parings encrypted with Delphic legends like Source and A/V Input. I also have two, count 'em two, remote browsers to wrestle with, each with a plethora of buttons that mean nothing to me. Sys Info. Guide Paging. A-B Zoom. Am I selecting a TV channel or docking the Mars Lander?

I don't know a lot about the workings of my two remotes, but I know this: should I press the wrong button, my TV screen will morph into a Strangelovian menu of options, few of which seem to relate to the planet I inhabit, and I will have to call my fourteen-year-old niece to come over and make it so I can watch *Seinfeld* reruns again.

I would like to report that radios have resisted the trend toward technological gobbledygook, but that would be false. I know because I bought a radio recently. It is a state-of-the-art Sony portable, a shiny silverish number that would not look out of place on the console of the Starship *Enterprise.* It features CD-R/RW Playback, a Digital Synthesizer and something called Tune Mode. There is also a small, significant looking window marked RX-D29.

I have no idea what any of this refers to.

The unit comes with a sleek, grey remote browser that I have never removed from its plastic bag. Why the hell do I need a remote for a radio? I can walk across the room to change the station.

I know the radio I should have bought—The Tivoli Model One. I saw a picture of it in a magazine this morning. It is plain, rectangular, about the size of a shoebox and features an On/Off button, an AM/FM selector switch and one large round dial of near-grapefruit proportions that you use to tune in your station of choice.

The Tivoli Model One has all the flash and pizzazz of a Ken Dryden press conference. No tweeters or woofers, no Auto Preset or Sound Virtualizer buttons. Apparently the boffins at Tivoli eschewed bells and whistles in favour of delivering good sound and an easy to operate design.

And while I'm handing out plugs for common-sense technology, let's hear it for the Jitterbug.

The Jitterbug is a cell phone, but unlike most cutting-edge cell phones you can't use it to text-message your golf buddies, speed-dial the pizza parlour or videotape your office party. It doesn't announce incoming calls with the first five bars of Beethoven's *Ninth* and it has no games-playing capabilities whatsoever.

It just does . . . phone calls.

Because it's not cluttered up with superfluous jabberwocky, the Jitterbug can offer useful functions, such as enhanced reception and an easy-to-read keyboard with finger-friendly buttons large enough to see and punch. It is also hearing-aid compatible.

The Jitterbug comes from GreatCall, Inc., a California company whose mission statement reads, "to simplify technology and make it available to everyone."

Music to my ears and solace to my technology-befuddled brain.

I see from my phone-book-sized TV guide that *Canada: a People's History* is being rebroadcast tonight. I'd really like to watch that, but the thought of trying to achieve TV liftoff armed only with two remote browsers formatted in Venusian makes me weary before I begin.

To hell with it. I'll read a book.

All the News That's
Fit to Click

*A newspaper . . . like a fish, should be consumed
when fresh; otherwise it is not only undigestible, but
unspeakable.*

—JAMES RESTON

So there I am, sitting on a park bench in front of the ruins of a tenth-century Moorish castle on the Costa del Sol overlooking the Mediterranean . . .

And I'm reading a profile of Canada's current PM Stephen Harper in that day's edition of the *Times* of London.

A miracle? Kind of. I was at the time deep in los boondocks of rural Spain—about eighty kilometres from the nearest Spanish city where one might reasonably expect to find an issue of any English-language newspaper. But here in my hand was an up-to-the-second edition of one of the best in the world.

It was, of course, just an example of the ongoing electronic revolution of the internet, a phenomenon that is transforming the world we live in. Fifteen years ago, a copy of the *Times* of London would have taken at least three days to reach me by post. In 2006 it's as close as the Print button on my laptop.

Closer even. I wasn't going cross-eyed staring at the flickering screen of a computer on that park bench; I was turning the pages of an actual newspaper.

I shouldn't have been surprised. After all, I live on a small island off the west coast of Canada. No bridges, no airport, no streetlights. On a good day I may spot bald eagles, sea lions, even a pod of killer whales. On the same day, I can stroll down to the corner store and pick up that day's edition of the *Globe and Mail,* the *National Post,* even the *New York Times.* I can be reading the same news story in the same newspaper at the same moment as a reader in North York or Yonkers.

Such an experience is about to get even easier. There's a company in Ottawa that's fixing to make it possible for you and me to walk to the corner, swipe our Visa or MasterCard through a vending machine and walk away with a fresh edition of just about any newspaper in the world.

The company is International Newspaper Kiosks Ltd., an affiliate of Satellite Newspaper Corporation, based in The Hague. What INK Ltd. offers is the chance to buy any one of 135 (and counting) different newspapers any time of the day or night from a friendly automatic kiosk near you.

And I mean different. Want to read the *Shanghai Daily?* It's as close as your credit card. So is *Libero Sports* of Peru, not to mention any of a host of papers in French, German, Italian, Spanish—even Iranian. These print-on-demand papers are updated throughout the day, just like regular editions of your hometown daily.

What the Kiosk honchos are homing in on is the comfort factor provided by an actual paper-and-ink newspaper as opposed to the rather sterile online virtual experience.

A couple of decades ago, in the heady first days of the brave new world of the internet, cyberspace gurus were confidently predicting the imminent death of newspapers. Dailies were doomed, they told us. People in the future would get all their news from their computer monitors. Pretty soon nobody would buy newspapers.

Well yes . . . and no. Millions rely on the internet for fast-breaking news these days, but newspapers haven't gone away.

The one thing the gurus neglected to notice was that reading anything lengthy on a computer monitor is a huge pain in the eye.

Computers are awkward, temperamental and hard to fold under your arm or stick in your back pocket. They are, in a word, uncomfortable.

Whereas newspapers are friendly. As Marshall McLuhan said, "People don't read newspapers; they get into them—like a bath."

Reading a real newspaper is a sensual experience. You don't have to sign on or log in to anything. There's no worry about passwords or Trojan viruses lurking in the background. All you need is an opposable thumb, a comfortable place to sit and a good source of light. And let me tell you, a park bench overlooking the Mediterranean ain't half bad.

Nope. Newspapers may have to do some fancy footwork, but they're here to stay. Because they're cheap, informative, entertaining and just plain reader-friendly.

Besides, you ever try to swat a fly with a laptop?

We're Next!

Invasion of the Body Snatchers, an old sci-fi cult movie from the fifties, is a classic study in paranoia. It tells the story of an alien invasion of our planet by mysterious human-sized seed pods. The pods show up in basements, in greenhouses, in tool sheds—even on a pool table. They take over humans one by one, but they don't kill them. They just turn them into walking, talking, emotionless zombies. In the last scene of the movie, the hero, who has watched his friends and loved ones turn into "pod people," is running down a highway, fleeing the menace. At the edge of exhaustion, he turns to the camera and screams, "You're next!"

Well, um, not to be paranoid or anything but, ah . . . we're next.

I refer, albeit obliquely, to the eerily named iPod, the sleek and sexy portable music player marketed by Apple and still selling like hotcakes.

The iPod is to the old Sony Walkman as a Porsche Carrera is to a John Deere tractor. A Walkman usually holds just one disc at a time. The iPod can hold thousands upon thousands of songs and still sit on your hip, as unobtrusive as a Fido phone. It even has a "shuffle" feature which allows the user to "randomize" his or her song selections. You become your own deejay. You create a sound track to accompany your life. This makes the iPod not so much an entertainment system as a body extension.

The iPod also allows users to connect to the internet, online music stores and other users. For serious fans, once they're in their iPod aural cocoon, there's really very little reason to come out.

Which helps explain those sleepwalking, head-bobbing, off-in-a-trance people I keep bumping into on the street.

Pod people.

Not surprisingly, dedicated iPodders are exhibiting some distinctively abnormal behavioural tics—especially when they are prematurely yanked away from their iPods. Sara Scalenghe is a Washington, DC, graduate student who was the victim of a recent burglary. The thief broke into her apartment and stole some cash, her digital camera, an heirloom gold necklace . . .

And worst of all, her iPod.

It contained her fifty favourite songs, a university course dissertation and several recorded conversations with friends.

"I know it sounds silly," says Sara, "but it changed everything. I was really upset. I can't explain it, but it hurt."

Scalenghe was so distraught that she even gave up going to the gym for her regular exercise. She couldn't bear to work out without her favourite tunes endlessly unspooling in her ear.

It was even worse for Washington accountant John Hoctor. A thief tossed his pad and made off with his digital camera, a laptop and an iPod containing more than two thousand songs.

Hoctor had spent weeks hunched over his laptop, transferring his extensive CD collection onto his computer's hard drive and then onto his iPod. All gone. "I have to start all over again," he says. And he doesn't look like he's got the strength to do it.

For those of us outside the iPod force field, the answer seems academic. Get over it. It's organized noise, for God's sake. But for people under the spell, it's pretty serious. Anita Boss, a forensic psychologist, says it's critical. "Everybody has a lot of memories they associate with music," she says, "and musical taste is usually very important to people. You actually have a piece of identity theft here. Anytime something is stolen that is so personal, victims are going to have a reaction like that. It's not the same as stealing a coat."

Well, I guess. And I guess it's not going to get better any time soon. Sony has just applied for a patent for a revolutionary method (developed for the blind and deaf) of beaming images and sounds directly into a person's brain.

I figure it will take advertisers approximately four-point-nine nanoseconds to glom on to this technology and apply it to the merchandising of mattresses, penis extension schemes and cough remedies.

Excuse me while I scream, "We're next!"

Time on Our Hands

A wristlet? Why, I'd sooner wear a skirt than a wristlet.

Such was the prevailing sentiment among manly men back in the early 1900s, when the devices first showed their comely faces. A girly thing for certain.

Wristlets—we call them wristwatches nowadays—were deemed effete and frangible, exclusively the preserve of elderly widows and swoon-prone damsels. When a real man wanted to know what time it was, he hauled a great honking gold watch the size of a hockey puck out of his fob pocket, popped the lid and took a reading, like Magellan sussing out the stars with a sextant. Fortunately *tempus fugit,* and customs, change. The wristwatch gradually shed its effeminate image.

And just as well, because the wristwatch is such a phenomenally sensible idea. So much more convenient than humping a bronze sundial around on your back or strapping an egg timer to your forearm and having to remember to flip it every three minutes. The wristwatch is lightweight, durable, accurate and quintessentially handy.

So why do we keep screwing around with it?

I'm looking at a newspaper ad for something called the Maxi Marine Chronometer, a product from Ulysse Nardin, a swanky Swiss watchmaker. The ad tells me that the Maxi Marine Chronometer comes with an official rating certificate issued by the Swiss Official Chronometer Testing Institute. It also says the device has a self-winding movement and a power reserve indicator and is water-resistant to two hundred metres. It doesn't say whether my Maxi Marine Chronometer will give me the time of day.

Overdone as it is, this watch is one of the more restrained models on the market. There are wristwatches out there that spew out barometer reckonings, compass bearings, depth readings and phases of the moon. Perpetual calendar? No problem. Built-in calculator? Stopwatch? Personal alarm? Lap counter? A dozen models to choose from.

See, here's the thing I want in a wristwatch: I want it to tell me what time it is and . . . er, that's it, really. I already have an alarm clock and a calendar. I usually know whether I'm headed towards the Arctic or the Antarctic, and I mostly don't care what the barometric reading or the phase of the moon might be.

As for my watch being accurate two hundred metres underwater—if my wrist ever finds itself that far beneath the waves, knowing the time of day will be the least of my problems.

I know I'm behind the times. Not like cousin Jeff, who's on top of everything, especially watches. He wears a Rolex on one wrist and a Patek Phillipe on the other.

Not that he's satisfied. The other day Jeff is walking through Union Station in Toronto when he sees a guy coming towards him, humping two huge suitcases. He also notices the guy is wearing a drop-dead gorgeous wristwatch on one arm.

"Excuse me," says my cousin Jeff, "That watch on your arm, it looks . . . special."

"My own invention," says the guy, setting down his suitcases. "Take a look." The stranger hits a button and the watch face shows Ontario, the major cities and the current time. "It's got time zones right across the world, plus I've dubbed in regional voice prints." He hits the button for Australia. The voice of Crocodile Dundee comes out of the watch and says, "G'Day, mate—it's quarter of six—last call."

My cousin Jeff is astounded, but the stranger isn't finished.

"Look at this," he says, and presses another button. A high-resolution map of downtown Toronto appears on the watch face, showing the subway lines, current traffic conditions and the score of the Blue Jays game going on down at the SkyDome.

"I have to have this watch," says my cousin Jeff.

"Oh no," says the stranger, "I'm still working out the bugs. But check this out."

He hits another button. An FM radio receiver in the wristwatch starts broadcasting a production of *Aida.* Another button displays the latest Toronto Stock Exchange quotations. Still another connects to Stephen Harper's backroom think tank.

Jeff blurts, "I'll give you a thousand bucks for the watch, right now!"

"Oh no," says the stranger, "I've spent more than that on it already."

"Five thousand! Ten thousand! Look," says Jeff, "I'll give you fifteen grand right now! Whaddya say?"

The inventor says, "But it's not . . . " Then he sighs, slaps his hand on the suitcases and slips off the wristwatch. Cousin Jeff writes a cheque, grabs the watch and starts to leave.

"Hey, hold on a minute," says the inventor, pointing to the two suitcases. "You forgot your batteries."

THE SHALLOW END
OF THE GENE POOL

Kids Will Be Kids—
If We Let Them

One of the most obvious facts about grownups to a child is that they have forgotten what it is like to be a child.

—RANDALL JARRELL

Ana Cross of Nanaimo, BC, would know all about that. Recently Ana was busted by a city bylaw enforcement officer for illegally operating a business on city property. The officer wrote her up and closed her down.

The business was a lemonade stand that Ana has been running by the road outside her house since she was seven. Ana is ten years old.

It isn't the bylaw control office that's at fault—they get a complaint, they have to act on it. What ticks me off is that Ana Cross has a neighbour so narrow-minded and flint-hearted that he or she derived satisfaction from siccing the law on a child.

For what—being too grown-up for her age?

Could be. Maturity and responsibility are not character traits we encourage in our young ones these days. According to an article in *USA Today,* many American schools have found a brand-new bogeyman—*red ink.*

School administrators have determined that the trauma of seeing a large, red X through a wrong answer on a test paper or examination might prove to be too "stressful, demeaning, even frightening" for the tender psyches of school-aged children. Teachers are being urged to go back to their Crayola boxes and opt for "more pleasant" colours such as green, orange or purple.

Concern for school kids' fragile sensibilities extends to the playground. The games of tag and dodge ball have been banned from several American schoolyards on the grounds that they are "too competitive." The principal of a Santa Monica, California, elementary school finds the game of tag particularly repugnant. "In this game," she says, "there is a 'victim' who is designated as 'It.' This creates a self-esteem issue."

Some educators say that all competitive sports, from soccer and baseball to marbles and musical chairs, should be tossed out in favour of "affirmative" sports like, well, pogo sticking, juggling and—er, that's about it, really.

If the folks at the Tufts Educational Day Care Center in Massachusetts have their way, kids will be preconditioned long before they even get to grade one. At Tufts, preschoolers are required to agree to a contract that reads in part: "I _____, know how to listen to my teachers. When my teachers talk to me, I will not scream, try to hit, or say 'You're not my boss.' If I do any of these things, I will go to the sensory loft so I can slow down my heart." Presumably each child will be appointed a lawyer with power of attorney since they won't yet have learned to read or write.

Don't feel smug, Canucks—things are just as goofy this side of the border. Not long ago, the North York Women Teachers' Association in Ontario published a brochure calling for the removal of "violent" and "militaristic" language in classrooms. The brochure replaces expressions such as "killing two birds with one stone" and "take a stab at it" with milquetoasty bromides like "getting two for the price of one" and "go for it."

Even the lowly computer did not escape North York Newspeak. The brochure urged teachers to instruct their students always to "press," not "hit" the computer keys.

If, like me, you think the brave new world of educational hypersensitivity is a little bit much, be of good cheer. We're not alone. Mrs. Sarah Goldberg of New York City is in our corner.

Each school day Mrs. Goldberg sent her son to a rather exclusive elementary school on Manhattan's West Side. And every day she sent with Jonah a cartoon of a smiling, spouting whale that she drew on the brown paper bag that contained his lunch. (The son's name was Jonah. Jonah and the whale—geddit?) Each morning, Jonah would put his lunch bag with all the other kids' lunch bags, and each day at noon, the teacher would distribute all the lunches. Because of the whale, Jonah and his friends knew which lunch was Jonah's and they thought it was very cool.

The teacher disagreed. Mrs. Goldberg got a telephone call from her son's teacher asking her to stop drawing the whale on the lunch bag because it was "unfair" to children with less pictogram-friendly names.

The next day, Jonah arrived at school with the usual whale-festooned lunch bag and a note to the teacher. The note read: "The Goldberg family whale policy will continue. Tell the other kids to get over it."

And for My Next Trick . . .

After looking at my family history, I've come to the conclusion that we Blacks have spent entirely too much time cavorting at the shallow end of the gene pool. We have a penchant for doing decidedly goofy things. Take Uncle Pinky. (Yes, Pinky Black. Don't ask.) Uncle Pinky is no longer with us, but his spirit lives on at our annual family reunions, where each year, sooner or later, someone will rise and relate The Cattle Prod Incident.

It happened decades ago at the Ontario Public Stockyards in Toronto. Uncle Pinky was a founding member of Black Brothers Livestock, Inc., a firm that acted as a middleman between farmers who wanted to sell their stock and firms like Swift's and Canada Packers looking to buy them.

One day, as happened from time to time, a cow lay down in one of the stockyards alleys and refused to get up, causing a massive traffic problem. When two tonnes of Holstein declines to budge, there's not a lot you can do.

Unless you're an innovative and forward-thinking chap like Uncle Pinky.

"Stand aside! Stand aside!" Uncle Pinky commanded the crowd surrounding the cow.

He must have looked like something out of a Buck Rogers B-grade movie. Uncle Pinky was wearing heavy insulated gloves and a leather helmet. He had a thick black coil of electrical cable wound around his body. One end of the coil was attached to a massive battery pack on his back, and the other terminated in a long steel wand that he held in his hand like a divining rod.

It was his own invention—the prototype for what may well have been the world's first electric cattle prod. One touch of the wand to the cow's flank, a modest burst of voltage, and the beast would undoubtedly spring to its hooves and be off and running.

"Stand back!" thundered Uncle Pinky grandly. He touched the wand to the cow's rump. The cow mooed once. And died on the spot.

Uncle Pinky always maintained the cow had died of a sudden heart attack, but everybody else pretty much concluded Uncle Pinky needed to fine-tune his cattle prod.

Bizarre behaviour runs in the family. I have a nephew who won a bet—and made the front page of the *National Enquirer*—by diving into a dumpster full of pig manure and coming up with an apple in his mouth. He came by such behaviour honestly. His dad once decided to see how quickly he could drive across Canada. Drove straight through from southern Ontario to southern BC for the last three days. When he got to Vancouver, he had to go to a doctor because he was unable to close his eyes.

Me? I've never done anything to match my colourful kinfolk, except maybe . . .

Well, there was the time back in the seventies when I won a balloon-tire bike in a pig-out contest.

A new restaurant had opened in town. As a get-acquainted advertising gimmick, the owners announced that they would give away a Schwinn Black Phantom to whoever could eat the most submarine sandwiches.

A Schwinn Black Phantom? All the free subs I could eat? I signed up. There were only six registered contestants on the day of the contest. After the sixth sub, there were only two—me and a bulbous chap who looked like he might just go the distance.

When I was halfway through my seventh sub, I hit a wall. I knew there was no way I could eat another one, but my opponent looked a little green around the gills as well. This called for strategy. I sang out to the proprietor, "Mmm, this is delicious! For my next sub, could I have extra salami and mozzarella?" My opponent clapped his hand over his mouth and bolted for the door.

I know, I know. Pretty lame compared to my nephew and his dad and especially to Uncle Pinky. Even lamer compared to Sonya Thomas. Sonya, who weighs forty-five kilograms soaking wet, won $9,200 in an eating contest in New York recently. She downed twenty-six grilled cheese sandwiches in ten minutes.

What's more, she patted her lips, pocketed the cheque and went right back to work her regular shift.

At a Burger King.

Sonya's a way tougher cookie than I am. I haven't touched a submarine sandwich in thirty years.

On Island Time

When you live on an island as I do, you learn to live without certain urban amenities most folks take for granted. Here on Salt Spring we have no ice rink, no Cineplex and hardly any drive-by shootings.

But that doesn't mean we're reduced to picking banjos and whittling on the porch till the sun goes down. We have some big-time diversions. For instance, who would ever have thought a place this size would have its own museum?

Well, we do. It's a living museum in the truest sense of the word. Because the man who built it—Bob Akerman—lives there.

And I mean *built it*. Bob felled sixty tall cedars, limbed and barked them, hauled them to the museum site (right beside his house) and put the building up. That was back in 1992.

Bob was eighty years old at the time.

Doesn't surprise anyone who's met him. He deserves at least a museum—if not an NFB feature-length film. There isn't much Bob Akerman can't do. Or hasn't done. He's the third generation of Akermans to call Salt Spring home. And his Salt Spring roots run deeper than anyone's I know. His paternal grandparents, English settlers, were on the island before Canada was even a country.

His maternal grandfather was an Irish expat who married—I am not making this up—an Indian princess. She was the daughter of Tusilum, chief of one of the Cowichan First Nations, born on Salt Spring—or "Chuan" as the natives called it. So one way or another, Bob Akerman's forebears have been on this island forever, give or take a millennium.

And Bob? Well he was born here before World War I and never lived anywhere else. He also, never in all those years, held down a regular nine-to-five, punch-a-clock-and-wait-for-your-pension job.

But he's worked harder than any three men I know. He's been a logger, a builder—cleared most of the roads on the island—a fisherman, a farmer and a sheep herder. At one time he had over a thousand sheep gambolling over Salt Spring's fertile hills and dales.

Oh, and speaking of fertile, somehow in between the logging and farming and shepherding, he and his wife Molly found the time and energy to raise eleven little Akermans.

Bob also tried his hand at land speculation over the years, picking up and selling off various parcels of land, but his timing wasn't always the best. At one time, Bob owned a kilometre or so of waterfront property on Isabella Point just down from Fulford Harbour. But he let it go. For three thousand dollars.

A kilometre of Salt Spring waterfront. Three thousand dollars.

Today? Well. Right now there's a thirty-six-hectare lot in the same area—Isabella Point. Bare land. No buildings. Some waterfront. Going for 1.49 million dollars. If you hurry.

Now that he's into his midnineties, Bob's slowed up a mite, but he's still keen to show visitors around his museum, with its Indian artifacts, photos, trophies and documents, not to mention wife Molly's thousand-strong doll collection.

As a matter of fact, it's a tradition on the island for classes of school kids to show up once or twice a year at the museum and listen to Bob talk about Salt Spring's past. And they do listen. Bob's a natural-born storyteller with a wicked sense of humour. A teacher I know says, when Bob starts to talk the kids' mouths fall open. You can hear a pin drop.

Some savvy outsiders must have seen that too. Back in the late seventies a film crew came over and shot a whole bunch of footage of Bob and some of his grandkids tending their flocks. Some New York TV producers saw the film, bought the rights and put it on the air. Which is how kids from Aklavik to Australia got to spend a few hours on a Salt Spring sheep farm via television. On a program called *Sesame Street*.

Thanks to his museum, Bob is still meeting and charming youngsters of all ages and keeping Salt Spring's past alive. Location? Hard to miss. It's about a three-minute drive from the Fulford ferry on your right-hand side. Cost of admission? One phone call. Bob likes to know when someone's going to drop in. He's in the book. Akerman, with a K. Hours of operation? Well, that's a little trickier. Bob's a free spirit. He's never had much truck with nine-to-fiving anything. As he puts it, the museum is "open when it's open and closed when it's closed."

Makes sense to us. We never have to change our clocks here. We're on Island Time, here on Planet Salt Spring.

Feud for Thought

Of all the weird and twisted viruses that can invade and infect the human family, is there any more weird and twisted than The Feud? My dictionary defines the feud as "a state of prolonged hostility or violence, especially between two families or clans."

Emphasis on "prolonged." The Hatfields and McCoys, two redneck extended families who lived in the backwoods of West Virginia, engaged in tit-for-tat murders for over thirty years in the late nineteenth century. Here in Canada, five members of the hated Black Donnellys (the adjective refers to character, not skin pigmentation) were beaten to death by their otherwise docile southern Ontario neighbours in 1880.

Not that feuds are exclusive to North America. The Campbell clan of Scotland, in an act of sublime treachery, wined and dined and then stabbed and filleted a whole roomful of unarmed MacDonalds in the massacre of Glencoe.

As a distantly related descendant of those poor, trusting, overly ventilated MacDs, I still twitch involuntarily when forced to shake the hand of a Campbell (especially if the first name is Gordon, like that of BC's premier). But perhaps I should try to get over it. After all, the Glencoe Massacre happened in 1692.

But even that seventeenth-century Scottish shiskabob is pretty small potatoes compared to what goes on feud-wise in the rest of the world. In large swathes of China, India, Pakistan and Southeast Asia, blood wars and vendettas are practically a way of life.

Nowhere more so than in Afghanistan where warlords and religious nutbars have been seething—and slaughtering compatriots, largely on the basis of their family affiliations—for centuries.

Still there is at least one small oasis of peace and tranquillity in the war-ravaged city of Kabul these days. The vicious and long-running Levin-Simintov feud is finally over.

It wasn't the largest feud in Afghanistan history. In fact, it only involved two people: Zablon Simintov and Ishaq Levin. And if you're thinking there's something oddly Semitic about names like that in an overwhelmingly Muslim country—you're right. Simintov and Levin are Jewish names. These guys were the last two Jews living in Afghanistan. This in a country that was home to Jews for more than eight hundred years and once had a Jewish population of forty thousand. By the time the Taliban took over in the midnineties, there were just Levin and Simintov.

And they hated each other's guts.

The two men—one a clerk, the other a carpet seller—lived in Kabul's last surviving synagogue—at opposite ends—and spent their days hurling curses at one another and planning various petty revenges. No one knows for sure what set them against each other, but their mutual loathing was absolute and non-negotiable. The Taliban arrested them both, threw them in jail and tortured them. Levin was convinced Simintov turned him in. Simintov was equally sure that Levin had ratted him out.

This was a feud that could only be resolved by death—and it was. One frigid morning, police discovered the half-frozen body of Levin, aged seventy, wrapped in a moth-eaten blanket inside his ramshackle apartment within the synagogue.

Was it murder? Had Simintov finally exacted the ultimate vengeance? Police thought so at first. They arrested Simintov and charged him with murder. But an autopsy of Levin's body showed that he'd died of natural causes.

Simintov won't be sending flowers. "The old man was crazy," he told reporters, tapping a forefinger against his temple.

Now that his arch enemy is dead, Zablon Simintov could cut himself some slack. There's nothing to keep him in Kabul. He lost his carpet business years ago and he's been reduced to begging visitors for money, whiskey and phone cards. He could leave Afghanistan and join his wife and daughters in Israel, where they've been living for the past six years.

But he won't. Ishaq Levin, his old enemy, has a son. Simintov is afraid if he leaves, Levin's son will take over ownership of the synagogue.

Milan Kundera, the Czech writer, once said that the trouble with hatred is that "it traps us by binding us too tightly to our adversary."

Sounds like he'd met Zablon Simintov. Or Ishaq Levin.

You Say Soy Latte,
I Say Double-Double

*I like Canadians. They are so unlike Americans. They
go home at night. Their cigarettes don't smell bad.
Their hats fit.*

—Ernest Hemingway

Ernie was just a young *Toronto Star* cub reporter goofing around on his manual typewriter when he tapped out those lines, but I think he was onto something. Canadians really are different from Americans. Look at how we order a cup of coffee.

The American-preferred, Paris-Hilton-sanctioned approach entails swanning into a fern-bedecked grotto strewn with overstuffed chairs and placing an "order" with someone who answers to the job description of "barista." You give the barista your order—say, a triple-shot macchiato with half-soy, half two-percent, a sprinkle of cinnamon and hold the foam. Then you sign a lien on your Volvo to pay for it.

And the Canadian approach? The Canadian—the true Canadian—shuffles up to the counter, lays down a loonie and mumbles, "Gimme a double-double."

Yes, I sing of Tim Hortons, or rather of the Milky Way of Tim Hortons outlets that bespeckle this far-flung land. Sturdy, glittering neon oases that beckon like alluring sirens to hungry, thirsty or strung-out Canadian wayfarers from Port-aux-Basques to Prince Rupert and from Whitehorse to Windsor.

Tim Hortons. I'm so old I can remember when the very first Tim Hortons opened—on Ottawa Street in Hamilton, Ontario. It was 1964. The Beatles were on *Ed Sullivan.* Khrushchev was getting the boot in Russia, just as Dief the Chief was here in Canada.

And at Tim Hortons you could buy just two things: a cup of coffee or a doughnut. For a dime apiece.

I'm even older than that—I can remember when Tim Horton was a man, not a coffee shop. A brush-cut, lantern-jawed, bullet-eyed defenceman in the National Hockey League was Mr. Horton. For seventeen seasons, he anchored the blue line for the Toronto Maple Leafs. He played pro hockey until his sudden death in 1974. He was killed in a head-on car crash, driving to Buffalo for a hockey game.

Popular all-star that he was, Horton still collected far more fans as an eatery than he did as a hockey player. By the late eighties, the franchise was offering drive-through lanes and a lot more than Dutchies and apple fritters. In 1988 the word "doughnuts" was quietly removed from all Tim Hortons signs. By then they were also selling muffins, hot soups, chilis and a whole range of "grab 'n go" munchies.

Not that they forgot their roots. Tim's place still offered doughnuts. Only now there were sixty-three varieties.

And the Canadian love affair with the name just kept growing. That single coffee shop in Hamilton back in 1964 was such a hit that they opened a couple more. By 1991 Tim Hortons executives were cutting the ribbon across the front door of the country's five-hundredth Tim Hortons restaurant. Less than a decade later, they opened Canada's two-thousandth outlet—in the year 2000, fittingly enough.

Ah, but what happens with all great Canadian innovations? Most of them—be they John Kenneth Galbraith or Pamela Anderson, the Canadarm or Canada Dry Ginger Ale—get sucked up and relocated in that giant capitalist corral to the south, the US of A.

And so it has been with the Tim Hortons phenomenon. It was

such a success it attracted the attention of the mega-giant Wendy's chain, which scooped it up in 1995.

An all-too-familiar scenario: US great white shark gobbles up Canadian minnow. End of story.

But a funny thing happened on the way to the cash register. The minnow turned into a man-eater. In the first quarter, the Tim Hortons franchise turned in sixty percent of the corporation's profit. Wendy's accounted for only forty percent. Now, Tim Hortons is expanding into the USA. As I write, there are 339 Tim Hortons outlets south of the border. Within three years that number will double.

And here at home, Tim Hortons is so entrenched it has entered the language. Grab a copy of the latest edition of the *Canadian Oxford Dictionary* and look up "double-double." It's defined as the way to order an extra-cream, extra-sugar cup of coffee.

As I write, you can order a double-double at any one of 2,723 stores in Canada. The company recently reported sales of $2.9 billion.

And it all started out with a hockey player. How Canadian can you get?

What's the Problem, Officer?

I once knew a radio sportscaster who was pulled over by the cops for speeding down Jarvis Street in Toronto. He still had a can of beer in his hand when the cop came to his window.

"I'll have to ask you to step out and walk a straight line for me," said the cop.

The sportscaster laughed. "[Bleep], officer, I couldn't walk a straight line."

He wasn't laughing the next day, but he was walking. For the next six months, after the judge got through with him. Still, I give him credit. At least he didn't try to bamboozle the cop with some lame-o excuse.

Traffic cops have heard them all. Bad enough they have to spend hours sitting in a cruiser by the side of a highway gnawing stale doughnuts and squinting at a radar gun while cars and trucks whiz by centimetres from their ears. On top of that, they have to hear the alibis.

I really had to go to the bathroom.
I didn't see any sign.
The accelerator pedal sticks.
I was late for a job interview.

No wonder they throw the book at us.

Mind you, some speeders are at least a wee bit creative. A highway patrolman in Illinois remembers the woman who blew through a red light at a major intersection. He flagged her down and asked her why she ignored the light. She told him she'd just had her brakes repaired, which had been very expensive, and she "didn't want to wear them out."

Ticket.

A British traffic patrolman chased a speeder for eleven kilometres, siren wailing, lights flashing, before the driver finally pulled over. He claimed he "hadn't noticed" the police car on his tail. Then he added, "I won't lie. I normally do sixty up here. I should know better. I ran over a woman last week."

Ticket. Followed by licence suspension.

A cop in Ohio remembers the attractive woman he pulled over for speeding one day. She also wasn't wearing her seatbelt. When he asked why, she said, "I'm an exotic dancer, and the seatbelt pinches my nipple rings. So I don't wear a seatbelt 'cause it hurts if I do. If you don't believe me, I'll show you."

The officer declined the offer. As did the traffic court judge, who found her guilty of speeding *and* failing to buckle up.

But my favourite speeder-versus-cop story happened right here in Canada. On the outskirts of Medicine Hat, as a matter of fact. Early one winter morning RCMP Constable Bill Wisen spotted a car pulled over on the shoulder of the Trans-Canada. The car was still running, but it wasn't going anywhere.

Constable Wisen pulled in behind the stuck car and walked up to the driver's window. He found a man passed out at the wheel and an empty bottle of Smirnoff's lying on the front passenger seat. The constable tapped on the window. The driver stirred and opened his bloodshot eyes to find:

(a) Cherry lights of an RCMP cruiser flashing in his rear-view mirror.

(b) A large, unsmiling RCMP constable standing next to his window.

(c) His powerful muscle car idling and ready to roll.

"Oh, [bleep]," the driver says approximately, slams the car into gear and floors it. The engine roars. The speedometer registers fifty—sixty—eighty kilometres per hour. The driver, white-knuckling the steering wheel, looks around. Incredibly the cruiser is still right on his tail and—more incredibly—the cop is still at the window, and he's not even out of breath!

The driver keeps it to the mat for another twenty seconds. The car and the cop are still there. "Pull over!" yells the cop. The driver's nerve snaps. He stomps on the brakes and turns off the key.

Which is when the driver discovers two important facts.

Number one: He's facing possible charges of DUI and resisting arrest.

Number two: His car is stuck in a snowbank.

There are hangovers. And then there are hangovers.

Mr. Peanut for Premier!

Consider, for a moment, the humble peanut. Not a pea, exactly, and technically not a nut either. A legume, actually, producing pods which ripen underground and give us crunchy seeds, edible oil and most divinely, my favourite self-contained food group: peanut butter.

That's not all we get from this unprepossessing little shrub. If it wasn't for peanuts, Jimmy Carter would have been unemployed before he moved into the White House. Peanuts also gave us, well, Charles Schultz's "Peanuts," the most successful and longest-running newspaper cartoon strip in history.

And then of course there's Mr. Peanut himself.

You know the gent I refer to? The elegant chap sporting a shiny black stovepipe hat, a cane, white gloves and a monocle? So dashing. So debonaire. So Fred Astaire—if Fred had the body of a peanut.

Mr. Peanut is the hardest-working employee of Planters Nuts, a division of Nabisco Corporation, and he's been on the job for eighty-nine years. He was the brainchild of a young school kid named Antonio Gentile, who, back in 1916 won a logo contest sponsored by Planters. Antonio sent in a drawing that eventually evolved into the familiar, dapper figure we know as Mr. Peanut.

The lad got five bucks for his efforts. The world got one of those rare capitalist icons that manages to transcend its grubby commercial origins to become a household name.

Millions of people around the world have warm and fuzzy feelings for Mr. Peanut, but Vincent Trasov? He's a little more . . . intense.

He *became* Mr. Peanut.

For the Vancouver artist it started off innocently enough, as a mere artistic diversion. Back in the late sixties he found himself irresistibly drawn to all things peanutty. He began collecting peanut memorabilia—peanut cufflinks, a Planters Peanuts coffee mug, T-shirts with peanuts printed on them. Presently he found himself making drawings, collages—even videos—all with a peanut theme. Then he saw a photograph of Mr. Peanut. Instantly he knew his destiny.

Over a period of months, the artist painstakingly constructed a full-sized papier mâché Mr. Peanut costume, right down to the white gloves and the monocle. Victor Trasov donned the Mr. Peanut costume in 1969. He wore it, on and off, for the next five years.

"When you're dressed like a peanut, you don't have an ego," says Trasov. "I could go down the street and give a performance in a top hat, monocle, spats, black leotards and tap shoes."

And he did. Mr. Trasov as Mr. Peanut tap-danced his way into the pages of *Esquire* magazine. He was featured in Andy Warhol's *Interview.*

Trasov-as-Peanut became a downtown staple in the city of Vancouver. He strolled through Granville Island to the delectation of the denizens. He posed for photographs with Japanese and American tourists in Gastown and Kitsilano.

He even tap-danced with a chorus line of vamps known as The Peanettes.

"I became a living sculpture and the city was my canvas," says Trasov proudly.

And not just the city. Trasov went international. As Mr. Peanut, he strutted his stuff in California, Oregon, Washington and New York.

The obsession grew. Mr. Trasov, a.k.a. Mr. Peanut, developed political aspirations. In 1974 he launched a "Mr. Peanut for Mayor" campaign in Vancouver. Dressed as his favourite legume, Trasov attended all-candidates meetings. He had lunch with the Vancouver Board of Trade. He became a local celebrity on BC radio and television.

Perhaps it was his defeat at the polls, or maybe the costume just became too claustrophobic, but Victor Trasov outgrew his Mr. Peanut obsession. He's still a well-known and successful Vancouver artist, but he's making it without the props of a top hat, white gloves and a cane.

A pity, really. A few more votes and Mr. Peanut could have been mayor of Vancouver. After that, who knows? An MP perhaps? Even premier of British Columbia?

Don't laugh. This is a province that's been led by the likes of Amor de Cosmos, Wacky Bennett, Bill Vander Zalm and Glen Clark.

Why not an actual nut for a change?

We Have Met the Enemy . . .

One of the great comic strips published in my lifetime—and yes, Virginia, there was a time when the juxtaposition of the words "great" and "comic strip" in the same sentence did not evoke a smirk—was called "Pogo." It ran in hundreds of North American newspapers from the forties until well into the seventies, when it's genial creator Walt Kelly called it quits. Both to life and to writing comic strips.

Pogo was the name of a whimsical, talking opossum who presided, loosely speaking, over an Evergladian swampland that featured a cigar-smoking alligator, a poetry-spouting owl and a pessimistic turtle named Churchy La Femme, among other unlikely and unforgettable critters. Mr. Kelly's MO was ingenious. His strip featured no humans, just animals. He gave them the gift of speech then let them comment on political events of the day.

Those animals said a lot of memorable things in the years the strip ran in the papers. One of my favourites came from the lips of Pogo, who, surveying some political debacle of the day, commented wryly, "We have met the enemy and he is us."

A pithy way of underlining the old chestnut that humans are their own worst enemy.

Not hard to prove. Was there ever a species on the earth that fouled its nest as enthusiastically as we do? From poisoned ozone to gas-guzzling SUVs, from pollution-strangled rivers to chain-sawed rainforests, we are not a class act, chum.

And we never seem to learn. The fabled Cedars of Lebanon are just a cliché from the Bible, destroyed millennia ago for ships' keels and—probably—firewood, leaving only desert where they once stood dark, green and majestic. Meanwhile, on the other side of the globe, Easter Islanders were chopping down their last trees to serve as log rollers to move their huge stone monuments.

Are we getting smarter? Can we pronounce "New Orleans"? A gorgeous city where for most of the last century, authorities drained and bulldozed about five hundred hectares of marshland—to sell houses. Marshland that nature had provided to protect against disasters like . . . oh, can we say "Katrina"?

We are dumb, no question. But maybe we're finally getting it. The London Zoo recently opened a new exhibit in a public display situated between the polar bears and the Siberian tiger enclosure.

It was called simply *"Homo sapiens."* It consisted of a large cage containing eight hairless, pink-skinned creatures dressed only in fig leaves, who chattered at each other and entertained themselves as best they could. People—the antithesis of a "Pogo" comic strip.

Sort of a day in the life of *The Simpsons* without the suburban trappings of Springfield.

The exhibit only lasted for four days, but it made its point. And it pulled no punches. The press release announcing the *Homo sapiens* display explained that it was meant to "highlight the spread of man as a plague species."

Maybe it's a good sign. Perhaps if we can publicly recognize the damage that we've done, we can turn it around and use our fabled ingenuity to actually heal the planet.

Maybe. But it's not as though we haven't known the score for some time.

I remember years ago when a travelling circus came through the small town I lived in. The circus featured the usual B-circuit offerings—a miniature midway with a merry-go-round and a carousel.

A Guess Your Weight gypsy, a Fat Lady and plenty of overpriced cotton candy.

They had animals too. Some chimpanzees, a boa constrictor and a mangy brown bear wearing a silly hat.

And there was one curtain behind which, for twenty-five cents, you could see the most fearsome creature on earth.

"This Way to See the World's Most Dangerous Animal," the sign read.

You paid your two bits, pushed your way through a moth-eaten curtain and came face to face with the most awesome, destructive beast ever spawned. For a mere twenty-five cents you could see this ravening beast in all his fearsome majesty.

In a full-length mirror.

Life Can Be a Ditch

He's an almost painfully average bloke, is Hugh Sawyer. A thirty-two-year-old Anglo-Saxon bachelor who works as a clerk in a large auction house in London, England. He starts his mornings, Monday through Friday, the way tens of thousands of other office drones do. He gets up, performs his ablutions, grabs a quick bowl of cold cereal, slips into a business suit and embarks on his dreary train commute to work.

Well, there is one small difference between Hugh Sawyer's daily routine and that of the rest of us. When you and I rise in the morning, it's usually from a bed in a bedroom.

When Hugh Sawyer gets up, he rolls out of a ditch in rural Oxfordshire. Really. Not even a tent. He has a swatch of tarpaulin he strings from the trees if it looks like rain. Otherwise it's just Hugh and the owls and other things that go bump in the night. He has a sleeping bag and a camp stove, some rudimentary supplies stashed in a couple of garbage bags—and that's about it.

Mind you, this is not a lifetime commitment from Hugh.

He only plans to do it for one year.

Why?

"I want to make people think about how much they consume

that is not necessary," says Sawyer. "I am trying to prove that it's possible to do everything you normally do, maintaining a full existence while cutting back."

I too have slept rough in my life, but seldom by choice and not for long. I've slept on the beach in Barcelona and in fields and woodlands through Scotland, England and France—but I had good excuses. I was young and stupid. And broke.

Later, when I became a working stiff like Hugh Sawyer, I went out of my way to make sure I had a roof over my head each night. But I remember running into a guy who thought differently. He was a producer at the radio station I worked for in Thunder Bay, Ontario. His idea of a good time was to grab a sleeping bag and go out and sleep in the backyard, sans benefit of tent. Just lying on the grass, looking up at the stars.

I remember thinking how odd it was that he was the only person I knew who would do that voluntarily. I remember also marvelling at how soft I'd become in a very short time.

Most of us have become pretty soft. Just a couple of short centuries ago, sleeping in a warm bed in a heated house would have been an uncommon luxury for the average Canuck. And who among us can imagine surviving a prairie blizzard or a forty-below cold snap with nothing but animal skins and a feeble camp fire for warmth? Native Indians did it for thousands of years.

Times change. We all live in tents now. Big, expensive tents—and getting bigger. The average new North American home is a bloated 680 square metres. That's fifty-five percent bigger than the homes we lived in back in 1970. Does an average family really need all that space? More important—can the average family afford it? I live in a one-storey, well-insulated home with a wood stove and a fireplace for supplemental heating, and I still smack my forehead every time I open my monthly heating bill. The poor doofuses living in three-storey suburban McMansions with four bedrooms and a heated indoor garage—how do they manage to pony up the dough to keep the place warm?

Japan has come up with a housing solution, but you're probably not going to like it much. Yamaha Corporation recently introduced MyRoom to the housing market. MyRoom is a shed, really.

A customizable, soundproof box that the owner can retire to when the need for a little solitude descends. The original concept was to provide a "privacy chamber" within Japan's notoriously crowded living quarters, but people are actually *moving into* their MyRooms. The units retail for approximately seven thousand dollars a pop, and they're selling like hotcakes.

It's not much better in Hugh Sawyer's neck of the woods. An "apartment" in London's Notting Hill area recently came on the market. It consists of a kitchenette, a shower stall and a closet—with a loft bed overtop. Total area: about five square metres. That's right, five square metres. And it's just been snapped up by a tenant eager to fork over thirteen hundred dollars a month to call it home.

There's an old saying that a house is not a home, but thanks to urban overcrowding, rising prices and shrinking prospects, sometimes a home is not even a house. And when the options come down to five square metres in noisy Notting Hill, a Japanese privacy cube or Hugh Sawyer's solution, I'd have to say that a ditch in Oxfordshire is looking pretty good.

A Flagon of the Grape

Well, the yuppification of Salt Spring continues apace. We not only have art galleries over here, a health food store, a tea room and a skateboard accessories store . . . we now have vineyards. Vineyards! About half a dozen of them last time I counted. I was lamenting these latest arrivals down at the coffee shop the other day to my pal Henry. He looked at me oddly and said, "What are you talking about? We've had winemakers on the island since the glaciers left. Don't you know Goodie Goodman?"

Well, I'd heard of Goodie Goodman. But I hadn't heard the half of it. I talked to a few old-timers and it seems everybody but me has a Goodie Goodman story.

Like the fellow who remembers looking for someone to clean his chimney way back in the seventies when Salt Spring really was a sleepy little backwater island. A friend gave him Goodie's phone number. He made the call and the voice that answered said, "Goodman's Funeral Parlour."

"I'm sorry, I must have the wrong number," said the caller. "I was looking for a chimney sweep."

"No, you've got the right number," said Goodie. "I also sell eggs."

Indeed he did. Goodie not only sold eggs, cleaned chimneys and buried departed Salt Springers, he also ran a service station, was the fire chief and drove the island's only ambulance.

Nobody knows how many heart attacks were suffered by moderately incapacitated islanders looking up to see Salt Spring's undertaker, in ambulance-driving mode, bearing down on them.

Goodie Goodman was also known as a fella who liked to hoist a few. The Harbour House Hotel was his favourite watering hole. Another old-timer told me he remembered having a beer or two with Goodie at the Harbour House. "I always left before Goodie," said the old-timer, "and Goodie always yelled out the same fare-well as I went out the door: 'Remember—I'm gonna getcha in the end.'"

As undertaker, Goodie was also in charge of issuing death certificates. A doctor from the old days remembers that going to Goodie's place to do the necessary paperwork could be a harrowing experience. Not because of Goodie's personality. He was nothing if not sociable. Maybe too sociable. The problem was you had to have a glass—or two—of Goodie's specialty: homemade wine.

"And that wine," says the doctor, "was vile. . . . One day Goodie gave me a tour of his morgue, and as we passed the embalming fluid vats a horrible thought crossed my mind. I turned to him and said, 'Goodie, please tell me you don't make your wine in these vats.'"

"And Goodie said, 'What are you worried about? It's a preservative.'"

I love to imagine an encounter between Goodie Goodman and one of Salt Spring's new winemakers. You know, the kind of folks who hold their wine glasses between thumb and forefinger and murmur knowledgeably about "amusing little burgundies" and "beguiling Zinfandels."

Goodie, though a yeoman winemaker, wasn't much on Winespeak. "I'll tell ya all ya need ta know about making wine," he once declared. "Yeast eats sugar . . . and craps alcohol."

The great thing is there's an outside chance I'll get to see that confrontation between Goodie and a wine snob one day, because despite being on Salt Spring since way back when, Goodie

Goodman is still with us. He celebrated his ninety-fifth birthday recently.

With a flagon or two of the grape, I trust.

Good on ya, Goodie.

Ouch! That Hurts!

There are more things in heaven and earth, Horatio,
Than are dreamt of in your philosophy. . . .
                                    —WILLIAM SHAKESPEARE

Indeed. One of the big differences (aside from a heartbeat) between Hamlet's close personal pal Horatio and your obedient correspondent is that I am acutely aware of how dumb I am. I fully accept that many terrestrial phenomena will forever remain a mystery to me. I will never fathom the intricacies of quantum physics. I don't expect to master conversational Urdu in my lifetime. Nor will I ever figure out the Byzantine kinks and curlicues of Michael Jackson's brain.

I will also never understand piercings.

Body piercings, I mean. Wherein a person voluntarily pays to have his or her carcass bored, reamed, stitched, drilled or stapled.

Yes, stapled. One of the latest piercing fads (that we can discuss in polite company) involves having large metal staples punched into one's body. I had a staple punched into my body once. In a rush to meet a history class deadline, I inadvertently—okay, clumsily—managed to staple the web between my left thumb and forefinger to a ten page essay about Samuel de Champlain. It hurt like hell when I did it and smarted for days afterwards. I can't imagine paying to have that done to me.

There are a lot of things about body piercings that I can't

imagine. Piercings and moi parted company thirty-five years ago when the Hollywood epic *A Man Called Horse* hit the movie screens. You haven't seen it? Lucky you. It's all about an itinerant Englishman, played by Richard Harris, who falls in with a band of Sioux Indians. He partakes of a tribal custom called the Sun Vow ritual wherein the devotee (Harris) is hoisted off the ground by means of ropes hooked through his pectoral muscles. Sound grisly? Looks worse. After I saw Richard Harris ratcheting skywards, howling and grimacing, I couldn't entertain the concept of an earlobe piercing, much less anything more visceral.

The thing that gets me about piercings is that they're so *useless*. All that agony and disfigurement, the swelling and risk of infection—for what? A safety pin through your eyebrow or a D-ring through your septum will not put you on the fast track to fame and riches. In fact the more flamboyantly visual piercings will shrink your circle of friends and limit your choice of professions, all of which will include the question, "Do you want fries with that?"

But with most fads there comes a tipping point at which said fad either fades away or morphs into something bigger. I believe body piercing has arrived at its tipping point, thanks to a young Texan named James Sooy. James likes to dream up new and different ways of attaching metal hardware permanently to his person. I haven't met him but I like to think he has the standard eyebrow ring, nose plug and chin stud. He may even have those ear plugs that make the bearer look like he's lugging around a couple of drink coasters in his earlobes.

What I know James Sooy has for sure is a tiny stainless steel barbell that runs right through the bridge of his nose. That's not so unusual. Lots of "mod" enthusiasts have nose bridge barbells. What's different about Sooy's barbell is . . . it's *threaded.*

Each end of the barbell has been carefully milled to receive specially modified screw-on eyeglass lenses.

That's right. When you and I put on eyeglasses we hook them over our ears. When James Sooy puts on glasses he screws them right into his head.

Is this dog gonna hunt? I don't think so. Sooy admits his invention can be a pain in the, well, nose. He says that to put them on or take them off is a ten-minute operation with a tiny screwdriver. I have to think that the market for a finicky gizmo like that is going to be deservedly minute.

On the other hand, chances are that pierced glasses will take off like a rocket. Even lead to other piercing innovations. How about a Timex spot-welded to your wrist? Your cell phone surgically implanted on the side of your head?

Don't ask me if pierced glasses will sink or swim. I'm the guy who once wrote that Leonard Cohen's singing sounds like a set of bagpipes being run over by a Zamboni. That same week he was named Canadian male vocalist of the year. I also bought Nortel stock and bet on the Canucks to win the Stanley Cup. Twice.

It's amazing I don't drive an Edsel.

Putting the Fan in Fanatic

Celebrity is a mask that eats into the face.

—JOHN UPDIKE

You know Agnetha? Agnetha Fältskog, the blue-eyed Nordic blonde?

Not ringing a bell for you, eh? Well, if you've been around the block, you certainly knew her once, although you probably wouldn't recognize her today. She's fifty-five years old now. Been living by herself on a remote island in the Baltic Sea for the past twenty-odd years. To tell you the truth Agnetha's gone a little bit weird. Afraid of airplanes. Can't stand crowds. Avoids open spaces. Doesn't like to be around electronic equipment.

Which is a switch for Agnetha. Back in the seventies, she was perpetually surrounded by thousands of people, not to mention television cameras, tape recorders and microphones. She flew around the world several times a year, first class.

Agnetha Fältskog was the Dancing Queen—the statuesque blonde in the Swedish pop group ABBA. She helped them sell 350 million records worldwide.

And it damn near killed her.

Agnetha developed celebrity phobia. She began to have nightmares about her fans turning violent and aggressive. "I had visions that [fans] grabbed hold of me," she says, "that I was being suffocated by the sheer weight of people."

Which wasn't so far from the truth. Agnetha remembers adoring fans at concerts surging around her like a stormy sea, reaching, clutching, pawing. "Sometimes when we were finally back in the car, we would burst into tears from the sheer terror of it. It shapes your whole personality."

Or warps it. Celebrity is a strange and wilful beast. Some recipients—Paris Hilton, Robin Williams—take to the spotlight like pot plants in a grow op. Others, like Agnetha Fältskog and Michael Jackson, wither and writhe like sausages on a hot barbecue.

And still others—a very few—jump out of the way before the celebrity express train runs them over. Take Charles Webb. He and his wife have spent the past forty-odd years living on the margins, taking menial jobs as fruit pickers, dishwashers—even janitors in a nudist colony. They didn't have to do that. Mr. and Mrs. Webb could have been living in a mansion in Beverly Hills, riding in limos and hobnobbing with the crème de la Hollywood crème at the Oscars.

Back in the early sixties Charles Webb, at the age of twenty-four, found himself an instant—and famous—multimillionaire. He had just published his first novel, *The Graduate*. It was about to be made into a blockbuster Hollywood movie, and the world was Charlie Webb's oyster.

He turned and ran. Forfeited all rights to the book and the movie, gave away two houses—even unloaded his wedding presents—and moved with his wife into a trailer park in England. "It [the wealth and the fame] felt phony," Webb says. "It just didn't work for us."

Was Charles Webb nuts? No. Rather brave, actually. "It wasn't slumming for slumming's sake," says Webb. "It was a need to understand something. And being short of money was part of it."

Fame can throw you down some strange corridors. John Cleese, once the Clown Prince of British comedy, wound up making motivational videos for small businesses. Cleese met everybody who was anybody in the entertainment business during his career, but even he could be dazzled in the presence of star power greater than his own. Meeting Queen Elizabeth for the first time, Cleese blurted, "I have seen you on stamps."

The famous baseball player Babe Ruth was a bit more phlegmatic in the presence of royalty. Upon being presented to King George VI at Buckingham Palace, Ruth nodded amicably and drawled, "How ya doin', King?"

That's the other thing about celebrity. It can puff up the ego, but it can let the air out of one's tires even faster—as Aaron Copland, the famous US composer, discovered in a New York bookstore one day. Copland noticed a woman at the cash register about to pay for a copy of his book *What to Listen For in Music* as well as a paperback edition of Shakespeare's *As You Like It.*

Copland touched her on the arm and asked with a smile, "Would you like me to autograph your book?"

The woman looked at Copland blankly and replied, "Which one?"

Goodbye Nursing Home, Hello Room Service

Long, long ago when dinosaurs stomped the earth and I was just a pup, Canada had a national treasure named Greg Clark. He was a wee spark plug of a man, a snowy thatch capping his five-foot-nothing stature, all illuminated by a leprechaun grin. Greg Clark was a newspaper man at the *Toronto Star.* ("You'll never get anywhere with all those damned little short sentences," he advised a colleague—named Hemingway.) And he served in the army in World War I and as a war correspondent in World War II.

He was also a teller of wonderful stories. Tales of Canuck soldiers in the muck of France, shopping for socks at Eaton's and fishing for trout in Muskoka. The stories appeared each Saturday in a newspaper supplement called *Weekend,* and I gobbled them up. The stories were wry and gentle, good-natured and insightful. Sounds corny, but Greg Clark made me glad I was Canadian.

What really intrigued me about the man, however, was what he did following the death of his beloved wife. Clark, then in his dotage—or as he would call it, his anecdotage—sold his Toronto home and moved into the King Edward Hotel. He took a single room, ate in the hotel dining room and entertained friends in the lounge.

To a white-bread kid marooned in the wastelands of suburbia such a life seemed impossibly glamorous. Imagine! An indoor pool and sauna! Twenty-four hour room service! Clean sheets every night! A uniformed doorman to keep the riff-raff at bay and a front desk clerk to field your phone calls and deflect Jehovah's Witnesses.

And never a dish to wash or a sidewalk to shovel.

It's hard to say which aspect of Greg Clark's life I admired most, the stories he wrote or his domestic arrangements.

Reality in the form of sceptical friends soon arrived to rain on my fantasy parade. "Live in a hotel? Are you serious? That would cost a fortune." Yeah, I thought, that's true.

But is it?

As I approach my own anecdotage and begin shuffling my worst-scenario old age options, they appear to come down to two. Nursing home? Or my own hotel room?

I've visited a few nursing homes, including some good ones, and frankly they're not that good. They are institutions and they feel—well, institutional. They also consist of just three classes of people: staff, residents and visiting relatives. I prefer more of a mix. The kind of mix you would find in, say, a hotel lobby.

And did I mention expensive? I did the math for a top-notch extended-care facility nearby and discovered it would cost me more than forty thousand dollars a year to live there. That's more than a hundred and ten bucks a day.

Plus it's academic, because they have a five-year waiting list.

Then I did the math on my favourite downtown Victoria hotel. It's sixty-nine dollars a day and I can take a room this afternoon if I want. The manager was cagey about how much he'd deduct if I moved in long-term, but I could tell he'd cut me some kind of deal.

And there I would be, ensconced on some of the primest real estate in the country, with free coffee in the room and a complimentary *Globe and Mail* left at my door every morning. Leaky roof? Not my problem. TV on the fritz? Have the front desk send up a new one. No parking? Who cares? Or rather, who cars? A line of taxis waits across the street around the clock, and a free airport shuttle leaves from the front door every hour. It can take me to several other hotels in the downtown area—or even to the airport where I can hop a flight to Cancun, Oahu or Kingston, Jamaica. All of which have similar cheap hotels.

You think it sounds a tad morbid and dreary, settling into a hotel room and waiting to croak? Hey, who said anything about waiting? Or croaking? I've got a plan. Check this little news nugget I found in *Harper's Magazine:*

> Average total cost for an American eighty-year-old to live out the last of his or her days on a luxury cruise ship: $230,497. Average cost to live them out in an assisted-living facility: $228,075.

That's right, folks—it's almost as cheap to live out your last years on a cruise ship.

And by the time I'm eighty, I'll have easily an extra two hundred and thirty grand, thanks to the forty bucks a day I'll save by living in a hotel instead of a nursing home.

"Taxi! Taxi!"

Earth to Arthur Btfsplk: Stay Home!

You old enough to remember Joe Btfsplk?

He was a mingy little guy in a black coat who appeared in the "Li'l Abner" comic strip years ago. He wandered in and out of the cartoon characters' lives, always trailing a black cloud with lightning bolts over his head. Wherever Joe Btfsplk showed up, bad luck was not far behind.

All of which is a roundabout way of introducing myself. Hello. I am Arthur Btfsplk, patron saint of hard luck travellers. Take a trip with me and you'll wish you'd stayed at home.

Take Spain. Recently I got back from three weeks' vacation on the *fabuloso,* world-renowned Costa del Sol.

I shoulda stood in bed.

Nothing against Spain. A beautiful country with a rich history and a vibrant culture, yada yada.

(Although the average Spaniard's grasp of English is *pathetic.* I could not make the Spanish understand me—even when I talked slowly and yelled really loud.)

Alas, the country and its people were not the problem. It was the getting to and from Spain that nearly did me in. Ten and a half hours each way on a jammed-to-the-wingtips airbus, surrounded by pungent strangers and sustained by infrequent snacks of mucilaginous goo of dubious provenance.

Me: "What's this?"

Flight Attendant: "Omelette."

Me: "What kind of omelette?"

Flight Attendant: "Lasagna."

It wasn't all claustrophobia and food poisoning. There was the inflight movie starring Don Knotts, which could be viewed on a twenty-square-centimetre screen mounted just on the far side of the beehive hairdo in seat 35B. There was the option of leafing through the suspiciously crusty inflight magazine. Or dozing off amid redolent fumes of Olde Worlde hair oil from the fellow passenger whose chair back, when deployed, hovered just millimetres away from my chin.

I know, I know—what a wuss! My ancestors came to this country riding steerage in vermin-infested cockleshell scows that took weeks to make the same trip. But my ancestors had an advantage— they were hapless peasants! They didn't know any better!

Whereas I was at all times painfully cognizant of the fact that back home I had my La-Z-Boy lounger, my lambswool slippers, an unbreeched flagon of Mortlach Single Malt, plus all-new episodes of *The Sopranos* awaiting my delectation.

It is always a bad idea for me to travel farther afield than, oh, say, the MacFrugals Outlet in Nanaimo. Such excursions always end badly.

Last year it was Mexico. I got sick, of course—that's a given. The insult is that I imperiously ordered the very meal that did me in. I tried to finesse the waiter with my Berlitz-Spanish-in-Five-Easy-Lessons expertise.

"Umm, especialidad de la casa, por favor."

The *camaron*—sorry, that's shrimp—the *camarero* rolled his eyes and disappeared. Two minutes later he presented me with a bowl of steaming, oily broth, the surface of which was broken by various lumps and protuberances, one of which seems to be the backbone of a small geckolike creature; the other, a baleful eyeball of indeterminate origin.

And that's how I learned the word *callos*—Spanish for "tripe."

It never goes well for me in foreign climes. I've been mugged in Majorca, pickpocketed in Paris, shortchanged in Chicago and rear-ended in Rotterdam.

But I think I may finally have learned my lesson. It came to me in a glorious epiphany at eleven thousand metres over Great Slave Lake on the return flight from Barcelona. I'd just turned down the lasagna omelette. The same Don Knotts movie was unspooling on the giraffe-friendly overhead monitor. We were all holding our feet up and breathing through our mouths out of deference to the passenger who was projectile vomiting from seat 21A.

The epiphany appeared in the form of a tiny little hologram standing on the chair-back table that was cutting off circulation to my abdomen. The epiphany—she looked kind of like Princess Leia in *Star Wars*—shook her finger at me and said, "Schmuck! Your name isn't Magellan—it's Btfsplk. You're a homebody and good at it. Stay there!"

Damn straight. That's where you'll find me from now on. Give me a call sometime.

Unless *The Sopranos* is on.

LAME AS A DUCK

Good News is No News

Nobody likes the bringer of bad news.

—SOPHOCLES

I once looked up from the crossword puzzle I was surreptitiously filling out to see my editor bearing down on me, paper in hand and thunder in his brow. Never a good sign.

"Yer supposta be the funny guy around here," he growled, tossing his burden on my desk. "Make something funny out of this."

It was a letter to the editor. A full page of sniping and whingeing about the shortcomings of our esteemed organ that boiled down to the old familiar lament, "Why don't you just give us good news stories instead of all the gloom and doom?"

The answer is simple. Newspapers don't lean towards good news stories because nobody this side of Ned Flanders could abide a steady diet of Pollyanna pabulum. Oh, there's nothing wrong with the occasional kitten-rescued-from-a-tree heartwarmer, but people buy newspapers to be titillated, outraged or appalled. It's a journalistic truism summed up in the brutally cynical editorial adage, "If it bleeds, it leads."

That said, I must admit that I too have had enough of forest fires, suicide bombers, carjackings, corporate crooks and ponderous editorials on the shortcomings of "today's youth." Herewith a three-flower bouquet of good news stories that didn't make headlines but should have.

Number one: The thong is dead. Is that not good news? The underwear thong, the single most uncomfortable, unhygienic and inadequate undergarment fashion in living memory is itself poised to become a memory. Sales have plunged twenty percent in the past year—and high time too. According to the fashion editor of the *London Daily Mirror,* customers, and particularly women, are giving the bum's rush to "the most ridiculous excuse for a pair of knickers since the chastity belt."

Good news item number two: An anonymous driver who pilots a city bus for BC Transit in Victoria, BC. This guy follows the same route five days a week. It's a route that takes him down suburban Ferndale Road past the house of James McDonough, aged ten. One very hot day recently, the driver noticed James sitting at the end of his driveway behind a card table holding a pitcher of lemonade and a couple of dozen plastic glasses. James looked downcast. Business, obviously, was less than brisk. So our driver stopped the bus, turned to his passengers and said, "C'mon, c'mon, lemonade for everybody."

The driver bought drinks for the house—or rather, the bus— out of his own pocket. A small thing? Sure, but it made the day for his passengers—not to mention for James McDonough, who was left with an empty pitcher and fourteen dollars in his cash box. His mom says, "James just thought it was the coolest thing ever."

Item three: The saga of Sheena and Willie. Firemen arriving at a burning house in Auckland, New Zealand, recently put a ladder up to an open upper-storey window, climbed through and found . . .

Sheena and Willie, struggling to get out. Sheena had the lead end of Willie's leash in her teeth, leading him towards the firemen.

Sheena and Willie are mixed-breed golden retrievers. Sheena is Willie's mom. Willie, her four-year-old pup, is stone blind.

Fire sergeant Ed Buck, who carried the dogs to safety, said, "They were both trembling but unhurt. They put a lump in my throat the size of a soccer ball."

The owner of the house, a fifty-nine-year-old schoolteacher named Harold Dean, said he didn't care about losing the house, "but these dogs mean everything to me. They taught me about faith after my wife died."

Turns out that Willie was born blind. The neighbours, family friends, even the local vet tut-tutted, murmured "too bad" and advised Harold and his wife Joan to save themselves a lot of grief and vexation by having the pup euthanized.

Joan said absolutely not.

She taught Willie's mom Sheena to be Willie's eyes. Joan trained Sheena to guide the puppy in and out of the house and around the yard by holding his leash in her mouth. Eventually Sheena was taking Willie for extended walks all on her own.

There was also a lesson for Harold Dean. "Joan died of cancer last year and I took it hard," Dean says. "Then one day I was watching Sheena walking Willie in the backyard, feeling sorry for myself when it hit me—that's what life's all about. Fidelity and devotion. It's what Joan and I shared during thirty-seven years of marriage."

"Self-pity blinded me, until these mutts gave me the eyes to see again."

There now. Don't say we never tell any good news stories.

The Sound of Silence

When you're 35, something happens to the music.
—GENE LEES

Thirty-five, huh? Let me see . . . I was thirty-five in 1978.

Yup, that was about when the music died for me. Pop music anyway. In the sixties and seventies I *owned* pop music. From the big names—The Beatles, Dylan, the Stones—to lesser-known private treasures like Jesse Winchester and Elizabeth Cotten, not forgetting Question Mark and the Mysterians. Back then, I knew the groups and the musicians who comprised them as if they were imprinted on my DNA.

In the eighties, not so much. The top ten filled up with names like David Bowie, Madonna and REO Speedwagon. They didn't do anything for me. I kept listening to my old records and tapes.

By the time the nineties rolled around, I was seriously out of it. My kids were talking about unfathomables like Lisa Loeb. Also Beau Jocque & the Zydeco Hi-Rollers.

I assumed Coolio was a sports beverage.

Today? Hah. I just googled "top ten pop songs." Not only have I never heard any of the songs, I've never heard of the performers.

So pop music has passed me by, or vice versa. But there's always serious music. Mozart never fails to cheer me. Beethoven can still make the hairs on my nape stand to attention. And the "Schmeisters"—Schubert, Schumann, Chopin—never stale.

Alas, serious music can get . . . too serious. Take John Cage. Please.

Mr. Cage was an American musical philosopher famous for the creation of a piece entitled "4'33"." It debuted at a piano recital for contemporary music in Woodstock, New York, in 1952. Here is a description of that first performance:

> *The audience saw [the pianist] sit at the piano, and lift the lid of the piano. Some time later, without having played any notes, he closed the lid. A while after that, again having played nothing, he lifted the lid. And after a further period of time, he closed the lid once more and rose from the piano. The piece had passed without a note being played and without [the pianist] having made any deliberate sound, although he timed the lengths on a stopwatch while turning the pages of the score.*

That's correct—the piece entitled "4'33"" has three distinct movements, none of which involves the creation of any music whatsoever. It runs exactly four minutes and thirty-three seconds, hence its name. A sharp-eared listener will perhaps hear pages turning, members of the audience coughing, the honking horn of a passing truck . . . and that's about it.

It's delightful to see how avant-garde music critics contort their prose into semantic pretzels as they try to explain the profound significance of "4'33"." They call it a seminal work, a revolutionary breakthrough, etc., etc.

None of them is laughing. Well, perhaps John Cage would be, if he was still around. (He died in 1992.) Add up the total number of seconds in "4'33""and you get 273. On the Celsius scale, minus 273 equals absolute zero.

Admirers are still performing and listening (?) to "4'33"" more than half a century after its first appearance, but John Cage was not one to rest on his laurels. He quickly put out another stunner called *Organ²/ASLSP*. The organ in the title is a specific instrument in a church in Halberstadt, Germany. ASLSP stands for, in Cage's quirky shorthand, "As Slow aS Possible."

And he wasn't kidding. The piece, all done with weights programmed to press on a specially modified organ at predetermined intervals, began its inaugural performance on September 5, 2001—with a year and a half of silence. In 2005, the piece moved on to *its second chord.*

If the universe unfolds the way John Cage envisioned it, this performance of *Organ²/ASLSP* should be wrapping up in the early months of the year 2639. That will be almost six and a half centuries after it started.

I googled John Cage too. It mentions that he wasn't just a composer, he was a passionate amateur mycologist as well. According to Google, he loved to roam the woods in search of wild mushrooms.

I'll bet.

It Was a Dark
and Stormy Night

It took me fifteen years to discover I had no talent for writing, but I couldn't give it up, because by that time I was too famous.

—ROBERT BENCHLEY

Some career advice to those among you who are Writing Impaired but nonetheless aspire to a career in literature:

Go for it. The fact that you can't cobble a decent sentence together should never stand in the way of your becoming a rich and famous writer. Harold Robbins couldn't write worth a lick, but that didn't stop him from turning out a string of bestsellers.

Grace Metalious was a horrible writer, but back in the fifties, she pecked out a potboiler that became the most popular paperback in North America in its day and eventually a TV series. It was called *Peyton Place.*

Ah well. Bad writing is like a low-grade flu bug—it's always going around. Herewith some wretched writing culled from essays penned by [sob] university undergraduates:

John and Mary had never met. They were like two hummingbirds who had also never met.

He was as lame as a duck. Not the metaphorical duck either, but a real duck that was actually lame. Maybe from stepping on a land mine or something.

The ballerina rose gracefully en pointe and extended one slender leg behind her, like a dog at a lamppost.

The dandelion swayed in the gentle breeze, like an oscillating electric fan set on medium.

Her hair glistened in the rain like nose hair after a sneeze.

He was deeply in love. When she spoke, he thought he heard bells, as if she was a garbage truck reversing.

And my favourite:

Her vocabulary was as bad as, like, whatever.

Nice to know the old literary standards are being maintained. I'm sure Edward Bulwer-Lytton would approve.

Bulwer-Lytton? The dean of bad writing. He was a contemporary of Charles Dickens, living from 1803 until 1873, and he gave us the very epitaph that epitomizes lousy lit. Edward Bulwer-Lytton is the man who penned the phrase, "It was a dark and stormy night." In his (dis)honour there is an annual Edward Bulwer-Lytton Bad Writing Contest in which scribes vie to create the single most inane, vapid, pompous and altogether ludicrous sentence of the year.

And now, confession time. I never understood why the IWADASN phrase was considered so execrable. I've read worse. Hell, I've written worse. It just didn't sound all that bad to me.

At least it didn't until I looked up the rest of the sentence Bulwer-Lytton wrote. The entire sentence reads:

"It was a dark and stormy night; the rain fell in torrents—except at occasional intervals when it was checked by a violent gust of wind which swept it up the streets (for it is in London that our scene lies) rattling along the housetops and fiercely agitating the scanty flames that struggled against the darkness."

Yup, that's bad enough to qualify Bulwer-Lytton as the patron saint of puffery.

Except.

I said that Bulwer-Lytton was a contemporary of Dickens. He was also, in his lifetime, *second only* to Dickens as a popular writer. And he wasn't always bad. Bulwer-Lytton gave us the phrase "the great unwashed." He's also the author who wrote that "the pen is mightier than the sword."

See? Just because you're bad doesn't mean you can't be great.

Dead Ants are My Friends

Blessed be the internet. My pal Dave Davies, way off in deepest French Creek, BC, sent me a sketch via email the other day. It's a simple line drawing of a pleasant-looking chap, shoulders rounded in supplication, head bowed, cap in hand.

"Thought you might like to see your namesake," wrote Dave.

The gentle fellow in the drawing is identified as "blessed Arthur Meek."

There is of course—*tant pis*—no Arthur Meek, blessed or bedamned. He is a misapprehension, a creature born of a line from a prayer misheard.

You know, the one from the Gospel of St. Matthew that goes, "Blessed are the meek: for they shall inherit the earth."

What do you call a mistaken creation like Arthur Meek? Well, we could say that he's a Mondegreen. That's what US writer Sylvia Wright would call him. She coined the term based on an aural mishearing she'd been carrying around for ages in her memory bank. Ms. Wright's misapprehension came from a Scottish ballad called "The Bonny Earl of Murray." She was especially moved by the final verse which goes:

Ye Highlands and Ye Lowlands
O, where hae you been?
They hae slain the Earl of Murray
And Lady Mondegreen.

As an adult, Sylvia Wright was continually frustrated in her attempts to track down the tragic legend of Lady Mondegreen. Her Scottish friends had never heard of her. The history books recorded no such person. The title does not appear in *Debrett's Peerage.*

Finally, some research into the ballad itself revealed the answer. Lady Mondegreen had not been put to the sword with her lord that fateful day. There was no Lady Mondegreen. What had happened was:

They hae slain the Earl of Murray
And <u>laid him on the green</u>.

Perhaps it was a heavy Scots accent that confused Sylvia Wright as a child. Or maybe it's just something about popular music that makes it susceptible to misinterpretation. Bob Dylan, hardly a splendid enunciator at the best of times, confused legions of fans who believed they heard the mumbling minstrel paying homage to expired insects. They thought the refrain from his anthem "Blowin' in the Wind" went:

Dead ants are my friends
They're blowin' in the wind.

Mr. Dylan is not the only pop music culprit whose mic technique and vocal stylings have led fans astray. In "Lucy in the Sky with Diamonds," The Beatles harmonize about "the girl with kaleidoscope eyes." A lot of listeners were sure they were hearing a medical prognostication. They insisted The Beatles were crooning, "The girl with colitis goes by."

In one of their biggest hits, Creedence Clearwater Revival sing ominously, "There's a bad moon on the rise."

But a lot of listeners heard instead specific directions that I've yearned to hear at all too many festivals, concerts and hootenannies, "There's a bathroom on the right."

Jimi Hendrix was legendary for the number of groupies he entertained, but he confused more than one fan about his sexual preferences when he stepped up to the microphone at Woodstock and crooned, "S'cuse me, while I kiss this guy."

"Kiss the sky" is what he said, folks. "Kiss the sky."

The odd thing about all these misheard lyrics is the vehemence with which the people defend their misheard versions. I once almost got in a fist fight with a guy who insisted that Crystal Gayle was singing "Doughnuts Make Your Brown Eyes Blue."

Come to think of it, I kind of prefer that to the original.

It's the same with my pal Dave Davies. He insists that "Blessed Arthur Meek" is a real person.

In fact, he's pretty sure he's a close personal friend of that rolypoly Biblical celibate, Round John Virgin.

The Duh Vinci Code

I don't know much about the guy or the woman sitting across from you on the bus, but I can tell you one thing. They're reading *The Da Vinci Code,* they're planning to read *The Da Vinci Code* or they've already read *The Da Vinci Code.*

This book, by the heretofore unheralded Dan Brown, is the most popular piece of processed tree since the Harry Potter explosion. *The Da Vinci Code: Special Illustrated Edition* sat for a while in number four slot on the fiction bestsellers list. This put it just ahead of the paperback edition of *The Da Vinci Code*—which was on the list not for weeks but for years.

The book is a publishing phenomenon. It has sold more than forty million copies—many of them right here in Canada.

Now I will tell you something about *The Da Vinci Code* that almost never gets mentioned in the book reviews. They never tell you how bad it is. I mean bad as in lousy, lame, unbelievable, trite, jejune and also wooden. This is the worst-written popular book I have ever read, and I was weaned on *Peyton Place* and Harold Robbins.

How bad is it? Here is the author describing a struggle between hero Robert Langdon and André Vernet, one of a blizzard of enemies

Langdon faces in the book's 489 pages: "Vernet turned to throw his full shoulder into the door, but this time the door exploded outward, striking Vernet in the face and sending him reeling backward onto the ground, his nose shattering in pain."

His nose . . . *shattering?* In *pain?*

And here is Brown describing Sophie Neveu, the romantic interest in the tale: "She was moving down the corridor toward them with long, fluid strides . . . a haunting certainty to her gait." Hmm. A hauntingly certain gait. What would that look like? As Truman Capote once said of another scribbler, "That's not writing; that's typing."

But the weirdest most unbelievable thing about this weird and unbelievable book is the time frame. Consider: Our hero— jet-lagged from a trans-Atlantic flight and exhausted from giving an evening lecture in Paris on religious symbology—is spirited off after midnight by the Paris police to a murder scene at The Louvre museum. He then becomes a Gallic version of *The Fugitive,* stealing a taxi and then an armoured van and later hitching a clandestine airplane ride to England while eluding the cream of the Paris *gendarmerie,* Interpol, Scotland Yard, the entire constabulary of Kent and oh, did I forget to mention the crazed serial killer albino monk? I am not making this up. Dan Brown is. Langdon scrambles from downtown Paris to a vault in a Swiss bank to a chateau in the French countryside to Biggin Hill airport in Kent to the King's College Department of Theology and Religious Studies in London (with side excursions to Temple Church and Westminster Abbey) and finally to Scotland.

And this all happens *in twenty-four hours.* Langdon doesn't take so much as a pee break, much less a nap.

I haven't even mentioned the most improbable scenario that kicks off the story. A world famous curator at The Louvre crawls about five hundred metres, hides something behind a painting, writes an invisible message in code, strips off his clothes and piles them neatly on the floor, lies on his back with "His arms and legs . . . sprawled outward in a wide spread eagle, like those of a child making a snow angel," and draws a cryptic symbol on his chest . . .

And dies. He dies because all this time he has had a bullet from a heavy-calibre automatic pistol buried deep in his belly.

A bullet fired by—you guessed it—one crazed serial killer albino monk.

So given a story with implausibilities big enough to pilot The Concorde through—why is *The Da Vinci Code* so popular? I think because it taps into one of the great boneheaded undercurrents of our time, conspiracy theory. The idea that Some Force Out There Has a Master Plan for All of Us. And Everything is Connected.

But Dan Brown isn't talking about JFK assassination theories or the Elders of Zion or Bigfoot aliens landing UFOs in crop circle formations that are really intergalactic greeting cards. No, Dan Brown's book is weirder. In a nutshell, *The Da Vinci Code* is an indictment of the Roman Catholic Church . . . for hijacking Jesus Christ.

You want the details? Read Dan Brown's comic book. But remember this: Mr. Brown is not a man to let anything as inconvenient as the truth get in the way of a colourful story. *The Da Vinci Code* starts with this sentence: "FACT: The Priory of Sion—a European secret society founded in 1099—is a real organization." This is the rock on which Brown builds his story. And it is a flat-out lie. The Priory of Sion was a sleazy public relations scam dreamed up, not in 1099 but *in 1956,* by Pierre Plantard, a French impostor, forger and self-confessed liar. You could look it up.

One last irony. Brown's profession before he wrote this clunker? English teacher.

Jesus wept.

Hear Ye, Hear Ye!

Dan Rather, venerable CBS news anchorman, hung up his headphones not long ago. And you would think from the news coverage that a king was abdicating, a literary giant had gone mute or possibly a pope had passed.

The man *read* to us, for heaven's sake. He put on makeup, straightened his tie, sat behind a desk and recited off a Teleprompter while pretending to look us in the eye.

This is not brain surgery. It is not even bricklaying. And yet Dan Rather in particular and news anchormen in general, have been accorded a status in modern culture just slightly below that of basketball wizards and Hollywood hunks. What is it about the anchorman? Why do TV networks line up to shower them with gobs of dough, drape them in Armani and Hugo Boss and altogether treat them like demigods—all for doing what our moms and dads used to do for free—namely, read us to sleep at night?

Actually I do TV news anchors a disservice. They not only have to read well, they have to look like a Ken doll while doing it.

Good looks were not a requirement in the radio business, where I spent my career. A radio newsman could look like Gollum as long as he had a good voice and didn't trip over his tongue.

And it's no longer entirely true that we worship at these guys' clay feet.

Ted Baxter changed all that.

The genial dope on *The Mary Tyler Moore Show,* who managed to mangle every newscast that long-suffering Murray Slaughter wrote for him, set the mould for the popular stereotype of news anchors. He had the big hair. He had the big voice. He had the big ego. And he was major-league dumb.

And Ted Baxter begat Jim Dial of *Murphy Brown* and Bill McNeal of *News-Radio* and Kent Brockman of *The Simpsons* and, most recently *Anchorman*'s Ron Burgundy.

Buffoonish blow-dried bubbleheads to a man.

There are a lot of theories about why we love to laugh at anchors. Adam McKay, the guy who co-wrote and directed the movie *Anchorman,* says "ultimately it's just about the hair." Well, I dunno about that. Admittedly Ted Koppel's hair is a wonder to behold. It looks like some bizarre sculpted shrub in the process of eating his face. And then there's CTV's Craig Oliver, whose hair tone shimmers between green and orange. And Peter Mansbridge, who is rapidly running out of anything to comb.

I don't think it's the hair. I think it's the fact that news anchors are authority figures, and as such, always good for a giggle. And let's face it, they ask for it. They look preposterously pompous, sitting all puffed up behind their desks with their solemn owl eyes and their chins tucked into their shirt collars to make their voices deeper.

Pompous? You bet. Listen, the most famous North American newscaster of the twentieth century, Walter Cronkite, actually had the *cojones* to end each newscast by intoning biblically, "And that's the way it is . . . "

No Walter, that's not The Way It Is. That's the way one TV producer and a couple of cameramen plus a scriptwriter agreed to say it was, based on the people they'd talked to and the film footage they'd managed to slap together over the previous twenty-four hours.

Luckily we don't have to work too hard at pricking anchormen's ego balloons. They do a perfectly good job of it themselves.

Such as the radio newscaster who legendarily signed off a

national broadcast with the words, "And that was the news from the Canadian Broadcorping Castration."

And my favourite: back in 1965, when the famous Black Muslim leader Malcolm X was assassinated, I happened to be in the control room during a radio broadcast in Toronto. Suddenly an out-of-breath news announcer burst into the studio, shouldered the show host away from the microphone and breathlessly told the nation, "This is an urgent bulletin from the CBC newsroom in Toronto. Malcolm Ten is dead."

Sorry, Walter, but I was there.

And that's the way it was.

Welcome to Blogworld

Some time ago I wrote about snowmobiles and why I happen to loathe them. I said that they were noisy. I pointed out that they were polluting. I mentioned that they were a pain in the butt (and the ear and the nose) for nonsnowmobiling folks who have the misfortune to live near overused snowmobile trails. I opined that snowmobiles were a noxious blight on what remains of our unspoiled winter wildernesses here in Canada.

Readers responded . . . enthusiastically.

I received two emails congratulating me on having the temerity to diss the powerful snowmobile lobby. (Hell, I didn't know there was one.)

I received two dozen emails and letters from dissenting snowmobilers taking me to task (in some cases justifiably) for inaccuracies and overstatements in my column—all pointing out what they perceived as my mistakes in firm but reasonable arguments.

And then there were the others.

I received hundreds upon hundreds of emails from a group which, for purposes of brevity, will henceforth be referred to as drooling, sub-moronic goons.

They were snowmobilers, too, I guess. Although from the

illiterate howls and schoolboy or scatological ravings, I have to assume they hired someone with a functioning brain to type the emails they sent me.

They called me every obscene name I have ever heard and one or two that were new to me—and I used to be a sailor.

They swore they would picket my public appearances and hassle my editors to get my column removed from newspapers.

Some even promised to come looking for me some dark night with tire irons and malice aforethought.

What made it even more pathetic is that someone in this Cro-Magnon fraternity forwarded my address to several snowmobile websites in the USA with the suggestion that they "swarm" me with responses.

And swarm me they did. The guest-book section of my website all but exploded with an infestation of grade-six-level filth and bile.

Welcome to Blogworld, where anybody with more spare time than brain cells can log on to the internet and trash the subject or object of their choice. No need to know the facts. No need to worry about fairness or objectivity. Just go online and vent. As CNN analyst and blog victim Jeff Greenfield says, the extra attention can be a good thing. Greenfield gets thousands of emails a week—many of them toxically abusive.

But he doesn't much worry about what he calls "the baked-potato brains who say you're a media whore . . . The freedom that it gives to anonymous twerps to spew out invective . . . that's just part of the process," Greenfield says.

Which is true. In Blogworld, everybody gets his or her very own column, and who's not in favour of democracy?

But it comes with a responsibility. If you use your space to talk potty mouth like a ten-year-old street urchin, you cheapen the medium and reveal yourself as a none-too-bright jerk.

I have no problem with legitimate criticism—the more the merrier. I don't mistake my pieces for Papal Edicts.

But for the sake of discourse—keep it reasonable. Keep it civil. And please don't threaten me. You look *really* stupid when you threaten me.

All I can say to the legion of legitimate and rational snowmobilers out there is—look around, folks. If this is the company you keep, perhaps you should consider switching to curling.

PS: This experience has left me with a new respect for thinking, reasonable snowmobilers.

But I still think those machines you ride are an abomination for the environment.

Two Pennys
for Your Thoughts

*Reading is an escape, an education, a delving into the
brain of another human being on such an intimate
level that every nuance of thought, every snapping of
synapse, every slippery desire of the author is laid open
before you like, well, a book.*

—Cynthia Heimel

*I honestly believe there is nothing like going to bed
with a good book—or a friend who's read one.*

—Phyllis Diller

Ah yes, books in bed. Not to come on like a frostbitten version of
Casanova or anything, but I joyfully confess to having passed a
good few hours over the past couple of weeks in bed with a couple
of Canadian literary lionesses.

And a lusty romp it's been.

What's more, both of these scribbling Canucks answer to the
name L. Penny—how unlikely is that?

Full disclosure: I've never actually, you know, *met* Laura Penny.
It's her latest book I've dallied with between the sheets. A book
called *Your Call Is Important to Us: The Truth About Bullshit.*

As for Anglo-Quebecker Louise Penny, I haven't seen or talked to her in more than twenty years. Not since we toiled together at radio station CBQ in Thunder Bay.

Her book has a much shorter title: *Still Life.* It's a murder mystery set in the Eastern Townships of Quebec.

Both books are grand reads.

Your Call Is Important To Us is what I like to call a smackhead book. You read it and smack your forehead, saying, "Damn! How is it possible that nobody wrote about this before?"

Simply put, the book is a furious (and hilarious) torpedo amidships for the leviathan bullshit industry. How is it, Penny wants to know, that we have so passively accepted the increasing tonnage of meaningless verbal and visual manure in our lives, from the robotic telephoney voice recording (that used to be a living, breathing human) to blathering politicians, Hollywood hucksters and outrageously deceitful advertising campaigns? Why have we let this insulting crap seep into our homes and our minds without fighting back?

Think of past federal election campaigns. When was the last time you truly believed anything coming out of any politician's mouth? Why do we just sit back like drugged lemmings and accept it without a murmur of protest?

Laura Penny doesn't murmur. She lets 'em have it with both barrels and a hockey stick across the back of the head for good measure. Advertising, public relations, the insurance biz, politics, entertainment, Big Pharma: "an all-you-can-eat buffet of phoniness" is what she calls the monsoon of mendacity that threatens to engulf us. Angry? You bet—but funny too. You'll howl with laughter as much as with rage when you read this book.

And then there's the other Penny—Louise. Her book *Still Life* is much more genteel, even though there's a full-blown murder front and centre. I won't give away the plot here, only tell you that unlike most dystopian fiction these days, the story is not gory or sleazy or twisted in the least. It's an elegant, rivetting whodunit crafted with grace and wit. And it's a dazzling evocation of daily life in the Eastern Townships that'll make you want to book a vacation there—preferably next fall in time for the annual striptease of the sugar maples. Bonus: *Still Life* begins with the most heart-rendingly honest preface that I've read in many a moon.

So. Looking for a little bedtime action? Here you go: two books, both written by L. Pennys. All Canadian. Highly entertaining. One hundred percent barnyard-droppings-free.

You're welcome.

The Art of the Headline

So what did you think of that headline?

Well, don't blame me, I didn't write it. I don't even know who did. Some ink-stained Gollumlike creature who toils in the bowels of the publishing house, I imagine. We've never met and probably never will. All I know about the headline writer is that I submit stories with enchantingly clever, deftly nuanced heads that perfectly sum up the topics I'm addressing in a handful of artfully chosen words . . .

And he, she or it changes them. Sometimes the new headlines are shorter than mine, or longer. But what really curls my snowshoes is—they're usually *better* than my headlines.

It pains me to admit it, but headline writers are the unsung Gretzkys of the publishing world. They are the playmakers. The setter-uppers. Let's face it—if the headline writer doesn't grab you, what would ever cause you to peruse my poor prose?

Which is not to say that every headline is a wrist shot through the five-hole. Some of them are downright bad. Or painfully obvious, such as the newspaper headline that informed readers, "Plane Too Close to Ground, Crash Probe Told."

Or the one that cleverly announced, "Cold Wave Linked to Temperatures."

But headlines can also be as deft as haiku and as clever as Leonard Cohen. How about this one, which appeared in the *New York Times* over an article about timekeepers at an all-male track meet? Over a photograph of several officials earnestly peering at their stopwatches: "These Are the Souls That Time Men's Tries."

Or this *New York Times* headline, which legendarily ran over a story about the actress Gloria Swanson. Apparently the New York premiere of a new Swanson film had to be postponed from Sunday to the following Monday due to a flash flood that had crippled the New York bus and subway systems. The headline writer's crisp summation: "Sic Transit, Gloria Mundi."

Would that headlines were always even half that subtle. Alas, with the sublime we often get the ridiculous—and the unintentionally hilarious. A California daily headline once informed readers: "Panda Mating Fails; Veterinarian Takes Over."

While a newspaper in Saskatchewan ran a story under a banner that read: "Red Tape Holds up Bridge."

Occasionally headlines appear that should be accompanied by an X rating: "Antique Stripper to Demonstrate Wares at Store."

And: "Astronaut Takes Blame for Gas in Spacecraft."

But you know whoever wrote this headline is no longer in the newspaper business: "Is There a Ring of Debris around Uranus?"

Personally I prefer the intentionally clever headlines over the accidentally hilarious ones. And no newspaper does it better than *Variety,* the bible of the entertainment industry. Over a story about how rural audiences were not attracted to Hollywood movies with rural themes, the *Variety* headliner wrote: "Stix Nix Hix Pix."

As Jimmy Durante might say, "It don't get suc-cincter then that!"

And just for the record, the *New York Times* is not always at the top of the heap when it comes to headlines. As a matter of fact, on one glorious occasion, the *Times* got its journalistic clock cleaned by the tiny upstart *New York Daily News.*

The news story broke in 1975 when then US President Gerald Ford announced that Washington would not be bailing New York

City out of its financial crisis. The *New York Times* weighed down its front page story with a headline almost as long as the item: "Ford, Castigating City, Asserts He'd Veto Fund Guarantee; Offers Bankruptcy Bill."

The *Daily News* headline writer said the same thing in six syllables: "Ford to City: Drop Dead."

Now *that's* a headline.

Virgin Ears for Vintage Music

I remember, as a tadpole in the fifties, lying on my parents' living room floor watching a dreary succession of unfunny comedians, corny musical acts and lame-o jugglers, clowns and animal trainers on a television program called *The Tommy Dorsey Show.* Typical Sunday evening in the 1950s.

But then.

Here is the host, Tommy Dorsey, introducing this weird-looking performer wearing a white sports coat and a duck-tail haircut. He has a guitar that he commences to flail as he begins to sing.

My life is changed forever.

I'd never seen or heard anything like it. I couldn't have been more galvanized if I'd stuck my privates in a light socket. Me and thousands of others. I was watching the TV debut of a musical phenomenon called Elvis Aaron Presley.

That was the big shock of that Sunday evening. The secondary tremor was the reaction of my parents, who were also watching. They hated him. They were angry, abusive even.

"What does he think he's doing, the clown," scoffed my father.

"Can't even understand the words he's singing," said my mother.

And my revelation, even as a chubby prepubescent was: *They don't get it.*

Flash forward a half century. A couple of kids I know are listening to some rapcrap on a CD from some guy named 50 Cent. "That's not music," I snort. "That's doggerel. And illiterate doggerel at that."

The kids' eyes roll in unison, and I have another revelation. *Omigod,* I think. *I've become my old man.*

Well, maybe. But let me introduce you—here in the sixth year of the twenty-first century—to David Zeke, a high school student who's not quite old enough to drink, drive or join the armed forces, but seriously into music. What kind of music?

The Who. The Beatles. Early Neil Young and vintage Dylan.

Music, in short, that's old enough to be his grandfather.

And it's not just David Zeke—all his buddies at Thomas Jefferson High School in Alexandria, Virginia, are into this Paleozoic rock and roll too. They've formed a group called the Classic Rock Appreciation Society. They meet every Friday afternoon to talk about and listen to the music they love.

Pink Floyd. Jethro Tull. Led Zeppelin.

"I'm a classic rock guy," says sixteen-year-old John Jaskot, one of the club members. "It all started in sixth grade when my sister played 'Bohemian Rhapsody' by Queen for me, and I was like: Whoa! I started going through my Dad's records. Now I listen to Jethro Tull with him. My whole family does—including my brother, who's six."

What about the current music scene? Hip hop? World? New age?

Not for these guys. You won't be hearing Eminem at a meeting of the Classic Rock Appreciation Society. Zeke's take: "The music industry has turned into a factory that's just churning out stuff."

John McDermott, a music industry watcher, agrees. "Music is countercultural again," he says. Kid's don't think it's their parents' music; they just view it as cool music that's not sold to them by MTV."

Such talk must be music to John Densmore's ears. Densmore is the man who played drums on Doors classics like "Light My Fire,"

"People Are Strange" and "Break On Through (to the Other Side)." And yes, he's still alive. And kicking plenty.

Multinational corporations have been knocking on Densmore's door waving multimillion-dollar cheques and begging for the right to use Doors songs as soundtracks to peddle real estate, pickup trucks and toothpaste.

Densmore's telling them all to take a ride.

"People lost their virginity to this music," says Densmore. "I've had people say kids died in Vietnam listening to this music, others say they know someone who didn't commit suicide because of this music." Recently Cadillac waved a fifteen-million-dollar offer under the noses of surviving Doors band members in exchange for the use of "Break on Through" to sell luxury SUVs.

Densmore told Cadillac to stuff it. "Onstage, when we played these songs, they felt mysterious and magic. That's not for rent."

Good on ya, Densmore. Thanks to geezers like you—and newbies like David Zeke—Neil Young may have been right when he sang:

"My my, hey hey. Rock and roll is here to stay."

Book Tours: a Fate Worse than Death?

The good news is that my book *Pitch Black* won the Stephen Leacock medal for humour. That made me pleased and proud. Stephen Leacock was a mighty funny man, and it's an honour to have my name in the same sentence with his, never mind winning the award that bears his name.

Now for the bad news. My book *Pitch Black* won the Stephen Leacock medal for humour. That filled my mortal soul with dread and loathing. Why? Because it meant a book signing tour couldn't be far away.

Being a writer is mostly a pleasant enough way to turn a buck. There's no dress code, no heavy lifting and no time clock to punch. But as with every job, writing has its dark side. Lounge singers get second-hand smoke syndrome; lawyers get lawyer jokes; cowboys who spend too much time in the saddle get hemorrhoids.

Writers get book signing tours.

Eventually the phone rang. I picked it up and heard the voice of my publisher. "Arthur," the voice said, "it's time to do a book signing tour."

And like an idiot, I acquiesced. Don't ask me why. A genetic flaw maybe. Authors almost always agree to do book signing tours, even though we hate them to a scribe.

What happens on a book signing tour is that the author gets to visit most of Canada's tiny dysfunctional airports where he or she will wait for flights that will whisk him or her to bookstores all over the nation.

En route the author will eat a great deal of quite bad food and spend many nights in dinky, airless rooms usually right over a motel pub that doesn't close until two a.m. That's when the fist fights in the parking lot begin. Around dawn, when the author is finally drifting off to sleep, the phone will ring. It will be the author's escort who's in the motel lobby, waiting to take the author to an early morning show interview.

Because it's not all signing books on the book signing tour. Sometimes there are painfully awkward encounters with local newspaper reporters, radio deejays or occasionally even local big-hair TV hosts. The interviews generally start with an off-mic confession from Big Hair: "I haven't had time to actually *read* your book . . . "

But eventually the author will fetch up at one or more of the local bookstores where a rickety card table and a treacherous folding chair have been set up. There the author will perch uncomfortably, and between chats with readers (if any), sign stacks of books. Bookstores like you to sign lots of your own books in hopes that the addition of your autograph will somehow encourage customers to take the plunge and buy a copy. They always have stacks of your latest books ready for signatures.

Well, not always. I remember the time I flew to Vancouver for the Word on the Street writers' festival. I did a reading that went quite well—people laughed, and no one threw anything at me—and at the end I flicked my trusty BIC ballpoint, ready to sign my name on the inside cover of a few dozen books . . .

And discovered there were no copies of my books. The bookseller had forgotten to bring them.

Could have been worse. British chick lit author Jenny Colgan says, "I've had my fair share of signing traumas. Sitting completely by myself at a desk in the main concourse of Stansted airport, 30 metres from the bookshop, directing people to their departure gates, is particularly burned into my memory."

Canadian author Margaret Atwood came up with what she feels is the perfect antidote to the dreaded book signing tour. It's a robot signer.

It works like this. The author sits in the comfort of his or her living room smiling into a video screen. Faithful reader in Jasper or Johannesburg, Kitchener or Katmandu, smiles into a similar video screen. The two exchange pleasantries. Reader places open copy of author's book on a pallet and asks for a special dedication. Author smiles and writes required dedication, with signature, still in the comfort of author's living room.

And instantly a robot arm clutching a ballpoint replicates the author's strokes into the copy of the reader's book.

"You don't have to be in the same room as someone to have a meaningful exchange," explains Atwood.

Well maybe. But between you and me I don't think Atwood's RoboAuthor is gonna fly. People who take the trouble to show up for a book signing don't want to chat with a video screen. They want to see the author in all his or her rumpled, frazzled, midtranscontinental-if-it's-Tuesday-it-must-be-Wadena glory. And I think we authors should stop whining and just suck it up. It could be worse.

We could be cowboys.

Evolution? Watch Your Mouth

*America . . . just a nation of two hundred million used
car salesmen with all the money we need to buy guns
and no qualms about killing anyone else in the world
who tries to make us uncomfortable.*

—HUNTER S. THOMPSON

Ah Mr. T., thou shouldst be living at this hour. Unfortunately
that option is not in the Tarot cards. Hunter S. Thompson
blew out his own brains in the kitchen of his fortified compound
in Woody Creek, Colorado, in February 2005. The drug-chugging,
gun-toting, invective-slinging colossus of Gonzo journalism, whose
motto was "When the going gets weird, the weird turn pro," finally
had to say uncle to Uncle Sam and throw in the towel. His country
got too weird even for him.

I'm sure the folks at IMAX know exactly how he felt.

You know IMAX? One of the great Canadian cinematic success stories. IMAX is to movies as the Brontosaurus is to the lizard
family, which is to say huge, unforgettable and famous around the
world. IMAX was the brainchild of three Canadian filmmakers who
got together after Expo 67 to work on a concept they called "giant-
screen technology." Simply put, they came up with a complicated
method of projecting a film on a screen ten times the size of a conventional movie screen.

Anyone who has ever seen the result will never forget it. IMAX films are drop-jaw gorgeous and incredibly lavish, with vertigo-inducing shots from helicopters and close-up encounters with wildlife and scenery that are enough to give cinema-goers the vapours.

If there's a knock on IMAX films, it would be that the scripts are *Reader's Digest* bland. They don't rock any boats. That's because IMAX films are inordinately expensive to produce. Consequently they have to appeal to the widest (read lowest-common-denominator) audience possible.

And that's the reason IMAX films never, ever offend anybody. Until now.

IMAX is in deep trouble south of the border. Theatres in several US states—including some theatres attached to science museums—are refusing to show several IMAX films on grounds that sound like something out of the Salem witch trials. The objectors claim that the IMAX films are blasphemous.

What sort of films are we talking about? Well, *Cosmic Voyage,* for one. It's an animated journey through the universe. Then there's *Galapagos,* a documentary about the famous islands where the incredible variety of wildlife led Charles Darwin to begin formulating his famous theory. And there's another IMAX film called *Volcanoes of the Deep Sea,* which is all about strange creatures that flourish near hot air vents at the bottom of the ocean.

Why have these films attracted the attention of America's self-appointed censors? Not because they use the F-word—you'll never hear that in an IMAX film.

It's because they use the E-word. They talk about "evolution"—and evolution is profoundly potty-mouth talk in George W. Bush's America.

The odd thing is, the USA has already had to sit through this movie. More than eighty years ago, the state of Tennessee put a twenty-four-year-old science teacher named John Scopes on trial for daring to teach Darwin's Theory of Evolution to his students. Famous lawyer Clarence Darrow defended Scopes and technically lost the trial, but he exposed the inherent inanity of the prosecution case and humiliated Scopes's prosecutor, William Jennings Bryan, to the point that Bryan actually died five days after the trial ended.

Where's Clarence Darrow when we need him?

Come to that, where's Hunter S. Thompson when you need him? Here's another Thompson quote:

> He knew who I was, at that time, because I had a reputation as a writer. I knew he was part of the Bush dynasty. But he was nothing, he offered nothing, and he promised nothing. He had no humor. He was insignificant in every way and consequently I didn't pay much attention to him. But when he passed out in my bathtub, then I noticed him. I'd been in another room, talking to the bright people. I had to have him taken away.

That's Hunter S. Thompson recalling his first meeting with George W. Bush at a Super Bowl party Thompson threw in Houston in 1974.

Where's the bathtub plug when you need it?

Extra! Extra! Read All About It!

The newspaper business is the only enterprise where a person is supposed to become an expert on any conceivable subject between 1 o'clock in the afternoon and a 6 p.m. deadline.

—ROBERT S. BIRD

Hah! That would be my one-time editor that Robert Bird was talking about. Miss Know-It-All. Miss How-come-you've-got-your-feet-up-on-your-desk-and-you-still-haven't-filed-this-week's-column-yet.

Couldn't she see that I was thinking?

What I was thinking was, what a cushy job she had with the big desk and the picture window and expense-account lunches. Nothing to do all day but browbeat terrified reporters and bullwhip the bleeding backs of faithful, underpaid columnists.

Nice work if you can get it. I wonder what her first job was—hall monitor on a slave galley?

Better than Warren Beatty's first encounter with a regular pay cheque. Beatty may have ended up as a Hollywood matinee idol but his employee origins were humbler. He started out as a municipal rat catcher.

A lot of celebrities began their working careers in less-than-exalted circumstances. Sean Connery started out as a milkman. Mick Jagger worked as a porter in a mental institution. Marilyn Monroe twisted nuts onto bolts on an assembly line in an aircraft factory. Madonna's first single? Probably a monotonous ditty entitled "Didja want fries with that?" She started out as a waitress in a burger bar.

But it's not just movie stars who rise from obscure origins. As a kid, Charles Dickens worked in a sweat shop producing tins of shoe polish. Abe Lincoln worked for tips as a hotel doorman. Tchaikovsky was in charge of paper clips in a dingy office.

Even dictators can start out small. Mussolini toiled in a chocolate factory. Hitler may have ruled the Third Reich and struck terror into the hearts of millions, but he began his working life designing posters for deodorants.

Speaking of dictators reminds me naturally of my editor, and of my very first job: editor and publisher of *The Humber Heights Gazette*.

That's right—editor *and* publisher. Me. Aged nine.

Well, why not? This country has a long history of newspaper moguls and tycoons. Max Aitken who became Lord Beaverbrook, Roy Thomson, Conrad (no relation) Black . . .

And just between you and me, being an editor—even an editor and publisher—is not exactly nuclear physics. I mean . . . look at my editor. But I digress.

I well remember the first edition of *The Humber Heights Gazette*. I drew it myself. By hand. I even remember the lead story. "Unusual Bird Seen on Rutherford Lawn," ran the headline. And below that was a picture—well, a drawing, actually—of what I am now pretty sure was an English sparrow.

True, I didn't have a splashy murder or a train derailment or an earthquake for that first edition, but that's the news business, eh? You go with what you've got.

Alas, it wasn't enough. *The Humber Heights Gazette* didn't make it. I had printing problems (my hand got tired). I had distribution woes (Tommy Farmer wouldn't let me use his red wagon). I had a shortage of advertisers . . . (well, none). And I was a little light in the personnel department (I was it).

In the end, *The Humber Heights Gazette* folded after just one issue. In fact, after just one copy of one issue. But it wasn't a complete disaster. Mr. Rutherford paid me two cents for that single copy. Perhaps he thought he recognized a sound investment. Or maybe he just wanted to read about the unusual bird on his lawn.

My career parabola seems to have run in reverse. I started out as a media magnate and press baron and ended up typing for beer money from you-know-who.

But you never know where Life is going to take you. Crooner Dean Martin started out selling bootleg whiskey. Steve McQueen? Towel boy in a brothel.

Wonder if my editor ever considered a career change?

The Wonderful World of Words

Words are, of course, the most powerful drug used by mankind.

—RUDYARD KIPLING

Wordsmiths—auteurs, literati, journalists, diarists and simple hacks like myself—are like Klondike miners. Every working day we roll up our sleeves, squat on our haunches and jam our metaphorical gold pans into the alluvial stream bed of our language. Klondikers dreamed of fat gold nuggets. We writers hope to sift through the dross and find—one day—the perfect word or phrase winking back at us in the sunlight.

Le mot juste, the French call it. But one can say many things better in French than in English. For instance, that moment when you think of the clever retort you should have made to the jerk who embarrassed you at the party, only now it's too late?

Took me twenty-seven words to explain that in English. French does it in four (two, really)—*l'esprit d'escalier*—the thought which occurs to you while climbing the stairs to bed.

But the French don't own a lock on linguistic precision. Even German, often considered a cumbersome tongue, can be deft. What do we Anglos call a person who leaves without paying a bill? We call him, er . . . a person who leaves without paying his bill. Germans have a single word for it—*zechpreller.*

If the contemplation of verbal vagaries tickles your cerebral cortex, run to your nearest bookstore and order a copy of *The Meaning of Tingo* by Adam Jacot de Boinod. Monsieur Jacot de Boinod has scoured the vocabularies of hundreds of languages from Sanskrit to Samoan, and he's served up a treasure trove of linguistic nuggets.

That utterly pointless gesture where we scratch our head as we try to remember something we've forgotten?

Pana po'o in Hawaiian.

That realization that the woman who looked drop-dead gorgeous from behind is actually drop-dead Gorgon when you see her face-to-face?

Bakku-shan in Japanese.

That unseemly scramble among press photographers and TV cameramen to get a better vantage point at media events?

The Chinese call it *Qiang jingtou.*

The uncontrollable habit of saying the most inappropriate thing at the most inappropriate time?

We call it "foot-in-mouth disease" in English. Indonesians are more precise. They call it *latah.*

Some languages have words and phrases for situations you can't even imagine arising. *Nakur* is a Persian word which refers to a camel that won't give milk until her nostrils are tickled.

Kualanapuhi is what Hawaiians call the poor sod whose job it is to keep flies off his sleeping king by waving a feather whisk. We'd just say "Dick Cheney."

And the meaning of *The Meaning of Tingo?* Tingo is from Pascuense, the language of Easter Island. It means to borrow things from a friend's house, one by one, until nothing is left.

On the other hand, some languages have words that cry out to be adopted, if only for their beauty. Say aloud the word that natives of Tulu, India, use to describe the sound of a pitcher filling with water:

Gulugulu.

Or the Indonesian word for the sound a doorbell makes:

Ning nong.

And how has our nation of Bob and Doug McKenzies managed to stay afloat this long without the Danish word *olfrygt?* It means "fear arising from a lack of beer."

So let's just adopt it. The beauty of the English language is that when we Anglos see a better word in another language, we don't moan with envy—we just steal it. Look at Canada. Half the country's towns and cities, lakes and rivers have names swiped from First Nations tongues.

My favourite example of lexicographical theft is not Canadian, German or Danish. It is Latin by way of British.

The story goes that General Charles Napier was commander of British troops fighting in India in the middle of the nineteenth century. Fighting under a handicap. He was expected to defeat his Indian foes in battle, but because of complicated politics he was under no circumstances to capture the capital of Hyderabad—the city of Sind.

Against orders, Napier and his troops took possession of the capital. He explained his failure and triumph in a one-word telegram to his superiors. It read, *"Peccavi."*

That's Latin for "I have sinned."

True story? Probably not—but a great one.

VENUSIAN
LIZARD KINGS

Paranoid? Who's Paranoid?

I get some weird Christmas presents from time to time, but this year I got the capper. It's a tiny swatch of leather with arcane symbols burned onto it, attached to a rawhide string that I'm supposed to wear around my neck. The woman who gave this to me swears it will protect me from "electrical pollution"—invisible fallout from cell phones, death rays from my computer, and toxic emanations from hydro wires, my microwave, my AM/FM radio, my toaster, my electric blanket and I suppose a battery-operated dildo, should someone give me one of those next Christmas.

I love the lady "gifter" dearly, but she is batty as a loon. She is convinced there is a vast Darth Vaderish conspiracy out there, the sole purpose of which is to poison us all. Nothing I say can sway her. No argument I mount can dent her force field of conviction. That's the perverse beauty of her paranoia—it's impermeable. She can twist and torque any data until it supports her belief system. No scientific proof? That's because all the scientists have been bought off. No media exposé? Whaddya expect, dummy? Big Media is just a mouthpiece for the Bad Guys. And if I argue too long, she gets very quiet.

She's not listening to what I say. She's thinking I might be One of Them.

It's a bizarre mind set. Scientists, police detectives—even reporters—assemble facts and try to marshal them to a logical conclusion. Paranoiacs begin with their conclusion and then cherry-pick and hand sculpt "factoids" to support it. It's the complete inversion of deductive reasoning, rationalism and—you know—sanity.

You'd like to believe that kind of juju superstition disappeared along with the Spanish Inquisition, bear-baiting and the sacrifice of pigeons to the Sun God, but you'd be wrong. It is alive and well in the twenty-first century. Exhibit A: The Aluminum Foil Deflector Beanie.

There are grown human beings walking around, bearing children, driving cars and casting votes who actually believe that wearing aluminum foil skull caps will deflect hostile radio signals. They contend that malevolent alien forces are beaming these signals at our brains in an attempt to achieve mind control over the human race. Recently, sceptical researchers at the Massachusetts Institute of Technology experimented with tinfoil beanies (I'm guessing significant volumes of beer were involved) and concluded that wearing such gizmos would, if anything, *amplify* any incoming radio signals, making the wearers twice as receptive to mind control messages.

At last report there had been no response from the beanie-o-philes, but no doubt they're coming up with a press release declaring the MIT report a blatant public relations cover-up attempt by Venusian Lizard Kings Who Would Make Slaves of Us All.

Or perhaps the paranoiacs of the world are losing heart. Colin Andrews certainly is. Andrews is Mr. Crop Circle. Over the past twenty years he's amassed more than thirty-five thousand photographs, 650 videotapes and hundreds of pamphlets, brochures and broadsheets, all purporting to prove that alien envoys are visiting earth regularly to stomp around in our wheat fields on moonless nights and leave indecipherable messages that are collectively referred to as "crop circles."

"Universal energy interactions may be at work and the interface between two dimensions register spectacular patterns of great meaning and such depth as man can yet imagine," muses Andrews.

Be that as it may, Andrews is now prepared to let his collection go—for a fee. It's for sale on eBay. Starting price: $250,000. So far, no bidders.

Hey, who wants to be lumbered with a cumbersome collection like that when the planet's only going to be around for another few years? That's the contention of people who follow the Mayan calendar. The ancient Mayans decreed that the world began on August 13, 3114 BC and will come to an end on December 21, 2012.

Of course, the ancient Mayans also believed it was a swell idea to carve the hearts out of living prisoners and to hurl screaming virgins into wells, so maybe we should take their prognostications with a grain of salt—but that's just me being negative.

I might also point out that the Mayans, for all their astronomical perspicacity, did not survive to see much of the eleventh century, much less the twenty-first. Mayan culture pretty much imploded around 1000 AD.

Well, what did you expect? They never had a chance.

No tinfoil.

Fads That Don't Fade

I 'll tell you how fast the world is moving. A short time ago, I had never heard the word "sudoku." Recently I googled it on my computer and found more than fourteen million sites. I checked again this morning. It had ramped up to over sixty-two million.

For those of you even more out of it than your obedient correspondent, sudoku is a numbers game that sprang up in Japan about twenty years ago. The word translates literally as "numbers singly." Players are faced with a box containing some random numbers, but mostly empty squares. (Stay with me, I'm not going to go deep with this.) The large box measures nine squares across and nine deep. Think crossword puzzle without the black squares. All you have to do is fill in the blanks so that each row and each column contains all the numbers from one to nine.

It's actually a bit more complicated than that, but that's as much as I can explain before my temples start to throb. Does this seem like fun to you? To me it sounds as appealing as a bout of avian flu, but sudoku has taken the world by storm. Just about every large daily newspaper now offers a sudoku puzzle in each edition.

Fads. There's no accounting for them.

Some passing passions are benign and easy to understand. I can appreciate the attractions of Nintendo, Slinky toys, Trivial Pursuit and Raiders of the Lost Ark-style fedoras. But what possesses people to crave Deely Boppers? Pet Rocks? Polyester leisure suits?

Back when I was a kid, raccoons almost became an endangered species thanks to the craze for Davy Crockett "coonskin caps." For several years, just about every North American under a metre in height sported a fake fur pillbox hat with a raccoon tail dangling over one ear.

Then there was the hula hoop. Who would've thought that a ring of cheap plastic designed to be twirled around the waist would tickle the imagination of millions? I don't know who did, but I'll bet he's one wealthy tycoon. Four months after the hula hoop first appeared in California in 1957, more than twenty-five million had been snapped up by eager buyers, many of them in places as far away as Japan, where it was known as the *huru hoopu*.

I never quite understood the draw of the hula hoop, but the fad that really baffled me was Rubik's Cube. This was the brainchild of a Hungarian sculptor and architect by the name of Ernõ Rubik. Back in the early seventies, Dr. Rubik found himself with too much time on his hands, so he invented the cube, a six-sided hunk of plastic made up of nine coloured squares set in rows of three. The squares could be rotated to change the configuration. Object of the exercise: to manipulate the beast until each side of the cube was just one colour.

Not too difficult, right? Wrong. Somebody figured out that the number of different possible combinations was a brain-paralyzing 43,252,003,274,489,856,000.

I figure if you put me in jail and replaced the cell lock with a Rubik's Cube, it would be approximately 43,252,003,274,489,856,000 years before I got the cell door open.

Unlike Shotaro Makisumi, a fifteen-year-old Japanese kid who holds the world record for solving the Rubik's Cube. He matched up all six faces of the cube in an astonishing 12.11 seconds.

I think of all the fads I've lived through, hula hoops and Rubik's Cube would be the two I would least likely spend any disposable income on—but here's the rub: they're both making a comeback. Hula hoops are showing up at music festivals and raves. So where do you buy a hula hoop these days? If you're lucky, at a garage sale. Otherwise you make your own. All you need is a couple of metres of irrigation tubing from Canadian Tire and a bit of duct tape (coloured electrical tape if you're feeling festive). There are even websites that will walk you through the construction.

And Rubik's Cube? Yep, it's back too—especially in Japan, where nostalgic thirty-somethings and kids grown bored with complicated video games are the big buyers. There's even a mutant version of the mindbender. It's called Rubik's Revenge. It features sixteen squares on each face.

So far I've managed to contain my enthusiasm.

Actually I'm okay with the reincarnation of the cube and the hoop. But if the sudoku puzzle knocks the crossword out of my newspaper, I'm going down to the editor's office to launch an official protest.

Wearing my coonskin cap and polyester leisure suit.

Nudes and Prudes

For me, one of the great pie-in-the-face moments for the execrable political correctness movement occurred on the steps of Toronto City Hall in the spring of 1991. That is when Toronto mayor June Rowlands announced, with a sniff and a huff, that she was cancelling the scheduled performance of an up-and-coming band in Toronto's Nathan Phillips Square.

Reason? The band's name. It was "unacceptable."

It was a hilariously defining moment for the careers of both Mayor Rowlands and the band. *The Barenaked Ladies* became instantly and internationally famous; June Rowlands was on her way to being laughed out of public office.

Now you would think a Keystone Cops-style boner like that would resonate in council chambers across the country. You would assume that public administrators from Carbonear to Qualicum would pause and look nervously over their shoulder before committing a similar civic bungle.

But no. Instead we have Mayor David Perry of Penticton. The city in the South Okanagan hit the headlines recently over a piece of publicly commissioned art that now stands in the middle of a roundabout at the entrance to the city's marina area. It's by a local artist, and it consists of a life-sized sculpture of a man holding a suitcase and surrounded by twenty-four other suitcases.

So far, so good. But curiously (and calamitously for Mayor Perry) the man is naked. Vienna could handle this. London wouldn't notice. Paris would yawn. Even Toronto the Good would get on board. But Penticton, if Mayor Perry's reaction is any indication, is on the brink of social meltdown. Responding to the mayor's objections, the artist *welded a square steel plate* across the sculpture's naughty bits.

This, of course, immediately focussed everyone's attention on the figure's midsection and made the whole work look ridiculous. But some people are more comfortable with ridicule than nudity, and Mayor Perry would appear to be among that number. "Penticton is not as open to such nude artworks as Toronto and other large cities," the mayor said.

If it's any consolation, nude prudery is not a Canadian phenomenon. Shortly after John Ashcroft was named US Attorney General, he ordered ten thousand dollars' worth of heavy blue drapes to hide a bare-breasted statue under which Attorneys General had been giving press conferences since 1936.

"The White House agreed to cover it up," quipped David Letterman, "so they got out one of J. Edgar Hoover's old dresses."

What is it about North Americans and simple, uncomplicated nudity? We can watch firefights in Fallujah in prime time, televised corpse counts from fire, flood and famine and NHL goons knocking out each other's teeth. But the glimpse of a breast or a buttock? Eek!

Europeans must just shake their heads. I am reminded of an interview with a French artist by the name of Louise Bourgeois, who was born in France but moved to the United States. The interviewer asked her to explain the difference in aesthetics between the two countries.

Mlle Bourgeois replied, "I'll tell you a story about my mother. When I was a little girl growing up in France, my mother worked sewing tapestries. Some of the tapestries were exported to America. The only problem was that many of the images on the tapestries were of naked people. My mother's job was to cut out the—what do you call it?"

"The genitals?" the interviewer asked.

"Yes," replied Mlle Bourgeois, "the genitals of the men and the women, and replace these parts with pictures of flowers so they could be sold to Americans. My mother saved all the pictures of the genitals over the years, and one day she sewed them together as a quilt, and then she gave the quilt to me.

"That," said Mlle Bourgeois, "is the difference between French and American aesthetics."

Not to mention Penticton.

If It Itches, Don't Wear It

I have never been known as a fashion plate.

As a statement of the obvious, that ranks right up there with Ralph Klein declaring he has never been recruited as a Chippendale model, but I want to make my fashion position clear before I introduce you to Simon and Jeremy. You need to know that my idea of sartorial splendour is baggy jeans, running shoes, my old high school sweater and a baseball cap of indeterminate vintage. I am, in short, a slob.

Happy hirsute hobo though I be, I would not go as far as the aforementioned Simon Wilkinson and Jeremy Stewart. They are a pair of popular young graphic designers working out of Toronto who have announced that their purpose in life is "to inspire more critical thought on the idea of clothes and their role in the construction of our identities."

When pressed to put it more succinctly, they explain, "We want to kill fashion."

Personally I find that just a little bloodthirsty. I have no interest in killing fashion.

But I wouldn't mind seeing it roughed up a little.

I've had a chip on my shoulder about men's casual fashion ever since the branding phenomenon surfaced a couple of decades back. Suddenly it became, well, fashionable, for major clothing manufacturers like Gap, Eddie Bauer and Roots to print their labels on the outside of the garment—sometimes in a banner headline right across the chest.

Wait a minute! I'm supposed to *buy* that overpriced Tommy Hilfiger sweater *and* turn myself into a walking billboard? For free?

That scam ticked me off. But not as much as it ticked off Simon and Jeremy. It's the very reason they started the GSSR.

GSSR stands for Grey Sweat Suit Revolution. That's what the aforementioned lads are encouraging us all to dress in, all the time—the classic hooded-top, elasticized-waist, oatmeal-grey sweatsuit most often seen in gyms and at the warm-up track.

Are they serious? Very. Naturally they have their own website—www.thegreysweatsuitrevolution.com—and they're recruiting apostles around the world. They've already mounted a grey sweatsuit installation in the display window of a fashion boutique in Toronto's trendy Yorkville district. In a couple of months they plan to have a full-blown show at the Museum of Contemporary Canadian Art.

At the risk of repeating myself, wait a minute! A Yorkville boutique? A show at the Museum of Contemporary Canadian Art? Isn't that an awful lot like, you know, *fashion* shows?

And what's this about recruiting role models? "When we had interest from a source in Los Angeles about extending the project there," says Stewart, "the first mission was to get a picture of Will Smith in a grey sweatsuit. The more pop culture icons the better!"

Oh yeah. Will Smith in a grey sweatsuit. Sorta like Tiger Woods in a Nike golf shirt. Or Wayne Gretzky in a Ford Taurus.

Don't look now, Simon and Jeremy, but you've been co-opted. You've cozied up to the very beast you sought to slay. I figure it's only a matter of time before I turn on my television and catch an animated version of Che Guevara decked out in a baggy grey hoodie and urging me to express my rugged individualism by running out and dropping a couple of hundred bucks on the "all-new, *no logo* sweatsuit!" (Naturally from FashionFreedomInc., A Division of WilkoStewart Enterprises.)

Thanks boys, but I'll pass. I'll continue to take my cues for what's in vogue from the late, great Gilda Radner, who once explained, "I base most of my fashion taste on what doesn't itch."

But Is It Art?

I was shocked and saddened to learn that Ilium lost his case in the Federal Court of Appeal.

Ilium—real name Brent McClelland—is a conceptual artist who lives in Calgary. He'd appealed to Ottawa to allow him to write off unpaid back taxes plus ten years' worth of living expenses incurred while he developed his theory of art.

His theory of art? Well, being a conceptual artist, Ilium had managed to boil it down to a single image, which he unveiled before the federal judges as Exhibit A.

It was an empty picture frame. Illustrates the decline of creativity, don't you see?

The judges gave Ilium a thumbs down, ruling that while a vacant frame may or may not be a work of art, it was something less than a viable business enterprise. Needless to say, Ilium was dismayed, as were his supporters, who called the ruling troubling. They said that judges should not determine what can be considered art.

Perhaps not. But I wish somebody would step up to the plate. I don't care if it's a CFL linesman, Stephen Lewis, Mr. Blackwell, Don Cherry—anybody but the bozos who currently tell us what is and what is not art.

Such as? Well, such as the London geniuses who awarded a recent thirty-five-thousand-dollar Turner Prize to British ceramicist Grayson Perry for his "seductive" pots. Mr. Perry—forty-three years old, 1.8 metres tall and married—showed up to collect his prize dressed as his alter ego Claire. Which is to say wearing a blonde page boy wig, a frilly blouse and a flouncy skirt à la Bo Peep.

Now I don't personally care whether Mr. Perry dresses up like Shirley Temple, Big Bird or The Incredible Hulk, but were his pots—glazed depictions of abused children, lacerated socialites and landscapes of "burned-out cars stalked by murderous moppets"—really the very best that the British art world could summon up in 2003?

I guess so. Perry's pots went on to be featured at London's prestigious Tate Gallery along with his closest competition, a bronze sculpture by the Chapman Brothers showing blowup dolls performing oral sex on each other.

I suppose such developments in the art world shouldn't be surprising—particularly not in Britain. After all, a recent survey of the five hundred most powerful people in the British art world—artists, dealers, critics and curators in museums and galleries—revealed that a majority of them (sixty-four percent) had a clear winner in mind when it came to naming the single most influential work of art in the twentieth century.

A Picasso perhaps? A Monet or Manet? A Matisse? A de Kooning? A Bacon?

No, it was a men's porcelain urinal, signed "R. Mutt 1917."

Granted, it was actually submitted to a New York art exhibition in 1917 by the famous French artist Marcel Duchamp. Simon Wilson, ex-curator of the Tate Gallery gushed, "It's got everything: rich metaphor, it's scatological, it breaks social conventions and it's very, very provocative."

You could render the same judgment about the Duchess of York breaking wind during a speech from the throne—but what's that got to do with art? Besides, whatever else the Mutt-Duchamp installation may be called, it is also undeniably a piece of plumbing that could appear on the wall of a *pissoir*. Where is the art? And how does Duchamp get to hitchhike on the coattails of some anonymous sanitary engineer?

What next—somebody wins The Turner for a triptych of Day-Glo painted VCRs?

I'll tell you what's next. In fact it's already happened. A gallery in Cape Town, South Africa, has featured an exhibit of famous seventeenth-century Dutch Masters.

Except all of the paintings are turned to face the wall. Visitors to the exhibit are confronted with row upon row of Vermeers, Halses, Steens and Rembrandts—as seen from the back. Curator Andrew Lamprecht says the reversal "forces gallery goers to reconsider their preconceptions about the art."

"These are fascinating things to see from behind," says Lamprecht.

Backs of paintings! Why, that's almost as brilliant and revolutionary as . . . as vacant picture frames!

Man, that Ilium! A genius just slightly ahead of his time.

Enough to Drive You to Drink

"**G**ood evening, Madame, welcome to EPIC Restaurant. Can I offer you something to drink? I have a splendid French Badoit, world renowned for its flowery bouquet and hints of the High Sierra, but if you don't care for artesian, I can offer you a premium glacial. I personally recommend the Gleneagles Natural. A transparently well-rounded libation imported from the heather-clad Ochil Hills of Scotland. It's a triumph of icy gusto with an astonishingly clean finish.

"What's that? You just want water with your meal? Madame . . . I'm the water sommelier. Water is what I've been telling you about."

Sounds like a dopey spinoff from a Monty Python skit, but it's true. There is an EPIC Restaurant—in Toronto's Fairmont Royal York hotel—and it does have a water sommelier. He's David Smuck. What's more, he can offer you everything from Welsh T Nant through Hawaii's Kona Nigari to Austria's Gerolsteiner and Italy's San Pellegrino.

And it is all bottled water. Not to mention big business. Internationally, 45.8 billion dollars big. People are lining up to pay for the privilege of drinking the world's most common liquid with an avidity not seen since the seventeenth-century Dutch tulip bulb craze.

After Americans, Canucks are the thirstiest per capita guzzlers of bottled water in the world. By the year 2000 each of us was chuga-lugging more than thirty litres a year.

Pretty impressive, considering that even the mainstream stuff—Dasani, Polaris, Evian—retails for more than the price of gasoline. What's really Pythonesque is that most of us—not counting those poor sods in places like Afghanistan and the Kashechewan First Nation—have an unlimited supply of the stuff on tap in our kitchens.

Ah, but it's not the same, you say. Tap water has chlorine and stuff in it, whereas bottled water is pristine and virginal, coaxed from glaciers or deep mountain springs.

Bunk.

Tests have shown that bottled water can contain at least as many contaminants as tap water, and in blind taste tests hardly anybody can tell the difference anyway.

As for the glacier ancestry, here's a tip. Coca Cola—which owns and sells the Dasani brand—gets its water from Brampton, smack in the urban heartland of Ontario.

And pointing at a snowy mountain crag depicted on the label of Nestlé Pure Life water, public health inspector Marilyn Lee says, "This water is from Guelph, Ontario. Have you ever seen a glacier in Guelph? It's misrepresentation . . . It's good water, but I live in Guelph . . . It's probably the same [as] water from my tap."

And perhaps not even as safe as tap water.

"Bottled water could have more bacteria, because it is disin-fected with ozone instead of chlorine," says Lee. "The ozone bubbles through so there's no residue in the bottom of the bottle. The chlo-rine [in tap water] is always there."

So how come every second person you see is lugging a canteen of bottled water, when they could be satisfying their hydration needs at the local water fountain? In a word: marketing. The same folks who convinced us that we craved a beer like Labatt's Lite (Labatt's Lite? Is there some beer aesthete out there for whom the taste of Labatt's regular is too robust?) have conned us into shelling out a fistful of loonies for what comes out of our taps for free.

It's a con job with a long-term price. Eduardo Souza of the Council of Canadians says, "The more bottled water we drink, the more we undermine public confidence in the ability of municipalities to serve water."

Not that you necessarily want to give government a blank cheque when it comes to liquids. Recently, Florida's then Secretary of State Katherine Harris strong-armed Florida state officials to adopt a "miracle" liquid called Celestial Drops, which she claimed could cure a canker disease menacing Florida's citrus crops. Celestial Drops came with a bafflegab pedigree worthy of the priciest item on EPIC's water menu. It was promoted as having "improved fractal design, infinite levels of order, high energy and low entropy."

And how did Celestial Drops come by these lofty credentials? Well, it "absorbed" them—by being stored in a holy room with sacred Hebrew texts.

Florida scientists ran an analysis and determined that Celestial Drops was actually—you guessed it—tap water.

The late, great P.T. Barnum observed, "There's a sucker born every minute."

I think we're picking up the pace.

Mr. Fix-It I Ain't

Not to brag or anything, but you are reading the words of Canada's next TV superstar. Really.

Say goodnight, Mansbridge and Robertson. Step aside, Ben Mulroney, ya little punk. Back off, George Stromboppaloppadingdong or whatever your name is.

Televisually speaking, I da man.

I'm about to land my own national TV series. It's a shoo-in for worldwide syndication. Life is good.

Best of all, I don't have to hump down to some cattle-call audition and try out for the part. I don't need to suck up to oily producers or memorize scripts. This one's in the bag. A Toronto production company called Propel Television is scouring the country looking for someone to star in their upcoming show called *Canada's Worst Handyman.*

Propel TV spokesman Chris Williamson says he's looking for a Canadian do-it-yourselfer "who takes pride in his handyman abilities, but really shouldn't." The kind of guy who, he says, "starts out with the best of intentions, but leaves a string of home-handyman disasters in his wake."

Chris, power down your BlackBerry, cancel those countrywide

auditions and start booking studio time. Your search is over. I'm exactly the guy you're looking for.

I possess in spades the three cardinal qualifications to be Canada's worst handyman. I'm a Canuck. I'm a klutz. And I have the tools. Lord, do I have the tools.

I've got vices and hammers, pliers and wrenches. I've got planes and chisels, hand drills and sanders. I've got screwdrivers: slotted, Phillips, Robertson and um, that star-nosed thingy. I also have saws: bench, sabre, radial, jig, band, crosscut, rip and hack.

And I've drawn blood—mine—with all of them.

Okay, maybe not the belt sander, but it gave me a nasty rash.

The one true sign that I'm a veteran handyman is what I'm packing on my hip even as I type these words. Yup, it's a Swiss Army Knife. Never leave home without it. I would have gone with the Leatherman except it doesn't come with a toothpick. In any case, the SAK is largely ceremonial. I haven't had it out of its sheath since the summer of '96 when I carved off the top of a knuckle trying to open a pistachio nut.

My house is a pathetic monument to my unhandiness. I've got a bathtub that leaks, track lights that flicker, floors that creak and dining room chairs that collapse like cheap Hollywood props when you sit on them. My baseboards bulge, my sashes sag, my drapery tracks droop and my storm windows let in the storms.

Ready for my close-up, Mr. Williamson.

Does my lack of any negotiable skills depress me? Are you kidding? It's about to make me a wealthy and famous television personality—what's to be depressed about?

The only possible competition I could face would come from Billy Bob Thornton—and he's automatically disqualified because he's American.

Which is just as well, because once you get past Thornton's undeniable acting skills, the man takes uselessness to a whole higher plane.

"There are so many things I can't do," Thornton admitted to a *Life* reporter recently. "I don't know anything about science or mathematics. I can't even turn a computer on. I'm not that smart. I mean, a lot of [bleep] is wrong with me."

Keep talking, Billy Bob. It's music to these tone-deaf ears.

"My girlfriend can barely get me to take a walk around the block with her," moans Billy Bob. "I don't like to go outside the house much. This could be Topeka, Kansas, for all I know."

I love this guy! He's still got the Christmas tree up in his living room because he's too lazy or incompetent to take it down. The thing winks and glitters in his living room all year long.

Providing, I guess, his girlfriend plugs it in for him.

And that's another thing Billy Bob and I have in common—staunch, loyal backup and support staff. I was all set to take apart the washing machine this morning when my Better Half swooped in and said, "No, no, that's all right, dear. I'll call the Maytag man. Why don't you . . . read the paper?"

Might as well get used to it, I guess. I won't have time for these petty fix-up jobs once I become a TV star.

Sign Here, Please

Would somebody please explain to me why every newspaper, magazine or flyer I pick up lately is telling me way more than I ever wanted to know about Paris Hilton?

Near as I can tell the twenty-something American heiress—I prefer heirhead—is on the world's celebrity radar screen because she is (a) rich (b) blonde (c) dumb and (d) er . . . that's it.

Lifetime achievements? Well, she did make that porn video with one of her boyfriends, which mysteriously got into instant worldwide circulation. Then there's her role in that TV show *The Simple Life,* in which she plays a rich, blonde, dumb urban princess who finds herself stuck out in the sticks. And she had a nice PR spike this past summer when she went online with a hysterical email offering a fifteen-thousand-dollar reward for the return of Tinkerbell, her kidnapped feral chihuahua.

She'd "forgotten" that she left the dog with her grandmother.

Oh yes, and her book. Mustn't forget her just-released literary opus entitled *The Tinkerbell Hilton Diaries: My Life Tailing Paris Hilton.*

Hmm. Fake kidnapping of dog named Tinkerbell closely followed by book launch of Tinkerbell "biography." Coincidence? Or is that the fetid odour of a desperate press agent I smell?

The book is a bestseller, natch.

Paris Hilton has, against all reason, become so famous that she is now trying to trademark her name as a logo—it's a tiny tiara with a stylized P in the centre of it. (P for Paris or Princess, geddit?) She plans to use the logo to brand her personal lines of fragrances, body lotions, bath gel, cosmetics—even footwear and kitchen utensils.

Martha Stewart, what hast thou wrought?

Am I the only one who finds it bizarre that a character model as dubious as Paris Hilton can be turned into a profitable marketing tool?

But then, why not? Robin Hood parlayed a career as a rural mugger into an immortal legend as a champion of the dispossessed. And we know that tomorrow's rising sun will shine on O.J. Simpson once again setting out on his endless quest to bring his wife's murderer to justice.

And O.J. armed only with a golf cart and a set of clubs.

Celebrity is an odd commodity. It makes no value judgments on the mortals it deigns to favour. Pete Rose said it best. Rose was one of the best players in baseball. He was also a gambling addict and he went to jail for betting on games he'd played in.

When he got out, one of the surprises waiting for him was an invitation to appear on *The Tonight Show.* After thanking Doc Severinsen for not playing *Jailhouse Rock,* Rose observed that despite all the records he set in twenty-three years as a major league player, he had never before been invited on the show. Then he turned to the studio audience and said, "You gotta go to prison to get on this show!"

Well, not quite, but it certainly doesn't hurt.

The downside of empty celebrityhood? Not much really. Both Paris and Pete have entered Celebrity Never-Never Land, where people are famous just for being famous. Neither will ever have to buy a drink or a meal again. And there will be rafts of invitations to parties and openings and galas. And endless doting admirers to fawn and adore.

Of course celebrities are expected to sign things a lot—autograph books, eight-by-ten glossies, posters, T-shirts. Pete Rose has probably signed more baseballs than he caught during his career.

Could be worse. He could be Ed Graham, the drummer for the British rock band The Darkness. Graham was doling out signatures at a press conference recently when he was confronted by a fan carrying a dog.

A stuffed dog. The tearful fan explained that the dog was the deceased pet of his grandmother, from whom he (the fan) was estranged. The only way the fan could achieve peace of mind was if Ed Graham would consent to sign the dead dog.

In an unusual location for a signature.

Graham explained it this way: "When [the grandmother] died, she left him the dog. He said, 'If you sign it, I might be able to make peace,' so I signed his testicles."

No doubt Ed used a ballpoint pen.

Advertising That's *Really* in Your Face

Marshall McLuhan once declared that advertising was the greatest art form of the twentieth century.

He should see what's happening to advertising in the twenty-*first* century. There was, for instance, a photograph in my newspaper recently of one Andrew Fischer of Omaha, Nebraska. Andrew is an average-looking dude, twenty-five to thirtyish I'd reckon, wearing fashionable horn-rimmed glasses and a tasteful, understated turtle-neck. He's got just a wisp of moustache and a tidy Vandyke goatee dusting his chin. Charming. Presentable.

And then there's Andrew's forehead.

His forehead carries a black-and-white slogan that reads, "SnoreStop. It simply works."

Those four words make Andrew Fischer's forehead worth fifty-five thousand dollars more than yours or mine.

Mr. Fischer, clever little entrepreneur that he is, has rented out his forehead as advertising space. SnoreStop, a company dedicated to muffling the nocturnal log-sawyers of the world, paid Andrew more than fifty-five Big Ones to keep its brand name up there, front and centre, for thirty days.

Brilliant idea? It certainly is for SnoreStop. Andrew's smiling face, with SnoreStop's banner emblazoned across the top of it, was picked up by the wire services and flashed to newspapers and television stations all over North America and Europe. The company has already garnered a million bucks' worth of free publicity with this little caper.

Not too shabby for Andrew Fischer either. Fifty-five thousand bucks is not exactly chump change for a young college student. And if he's like the rest of us, he probably didn't have any conflicting plans for his forehead for the next month or so anyway.

It's amazing what inventive types can come up with just by using their, well, heads. Take Frank J. Smith of Orlando, Florida. Frank is the proud possessor of US patent number 4,022,227.

His statement of claim reads, "A method for styling hair to cover bald areas using only the individual's own hair, comprising separating the hair on the head into several substantially equal sections, taking the hair on one section and placing it over the bald area, then taking the hair on another section and placing it over the first section, and finally taking . . . "

Well, you get the idea. Frank. J. Smith filed a patent giving him exclusive ownership of the comb-over, that lame and desperate camouflage gambit deployed by balding men trying to convince themselves that they're really not losing hair.

Lucky for comb-over giants like Pierre Berton and René Lévesque that they're no longer with us. Presumably Frank J. Smith of Orlando, Florida, would be slapping them with patent infringement lawsuits.

Moral of the story? Even a bad idea—and believe me, men, comb-overs are *always* a bad idea; those wispy strands of filament plastered across your burgeoning pinkness make you look like a walking bar code—can be a moneymaker for somebody.

Which brings us back to Andrew Fischer and his forehead-as-billboard concept. Now that's what I call a *great* idea. Even greater for me than for Andrew.

See, Andrew has what is known in the barbering business as a high forehead. The SnoreStop pitch fits snugly in between his eyebrows and his hairline.

I, on the other hand, as a chrome dome of some decades' standing, am pretty much *all* forehead. Andrew gets four words on his ah, billboard. I could print the Sunday edition of the *Toronto Star* on my noggin and still have room left over for a Thought for the Day and the first four verses of "O Canada." In English and French.

This could be my big break, folks. Wish me luck. Tell your friends.

This space for rent.

Bionic Manhood? No Thanks

You don't think Canadians are fascinating? Check this guy out. There he stands, dressed only in his skivvies, slathering his body with Vaseline. That's so he can slide into his most prized possession.

The Ursus Mark VII is an armoured body suit that makes the wearer look like the Michelin Man. Ursus Mark VII is composed of shark-proof chain mesh, reinforced steel plates and extremely high-impact plastic. It contains an air-conditioning unit, protective airbags and robotic arms, not to mention a built-in computer and a video screen.

The guy in his underwear—Troy Hurtubise, from North Bay, Ontario—hopes the Ursus Mark VII is rugged enough to withstand an attack from an enraged grizzly. His hope is especially fervent because he expects to be inside the suit when the grizzly attacks.

Hurtubise claims he has spent more than sixteen hundred hours and two hundred thousand dollars of his own money on this Robocop-style antibear suit. Does this make him a certifiable nut-bar? Not necessarily. Chances are Hurtubise is a man ahead of his time.

Consider what is going on at the University of Tsukuba near

Tokyo. Scientists there are working on something that could put you, me and your great-uncle Virgil in the backfield of the Hamilton Tiger Cats next season.

It's a motorized body frame called the Hybrid Assistive Limb that fits over the human carcass—yours, mine, Uncle Virgil's—like a scaled-down version of the Ursus Mark VII. This exoskeleton receives electronic signals from sensors attached to the wearer's skin. When your brain says "left knee—bend!" a microprocessor in the body frame transmits the thought as an electrical impulse to miniature motors located at the left knee joint and lo, your left knee is bending.

And not only knees, but hips and ankles, elbows, wrists and pinkie fingers. And not just simple bending but flexing, torquing, springing and clenching—at superhuman strength levels. Doesn't matter if the actual human joint is arthritic, rheumatic, sclerotic or flapping like a batwing saloon door. The exoskeleton does all the work and provides all the power. The Hybrid Assistive Limb has the potential to turn a thirty-six kilogram anorectic into Silken Laumann and Preston Manning into The Incredible Hulk.

Note the word "potential." The Hybrid Assistive Limb isn't there yet. Even though the Japanese boffins have spent more than a hundred million yen on the project so far, their prototype still weighs in at close to eighteen kilograms, which is a lot more than most of us would be comfortable hauling around. But they're working on it. The head researcher, Dr. Yoshiyuki Sankai, says his ultimate aim is to make a device that's thin and comfortable enough for anyone to wear.

The ramifications are stupendous. Couch potatoes like you and me could be Olympic contenders. Brittle octogenarians could dance like Fred Astaire and Ginger Rogers. We could all take the stairs up the CN Tower two at a time. The lion would lie down with the retrofitted lamb, and the lamb would whup Leo at arm wrestling in three seconds flat.

The only question remaining is, do we really want this?

The famous Riddle of the Sphinx in Greek mythology asks, "What goes on four legs in the morning, two legs at noon and three legs in the evening?" The answer, as clever Oedipus divined, is man himself. A man crawls in childhood, stands erect at maturity and typically hobbles off to his reward clutching his third leg—a cane.

Humankind followed that biological arc pretty consistently since our forebears first wriggled out of the primordial ooze a few million years ago. It feels right and it works well. As a chap on the cusp of the three-legged stage, I thoroughly enjoy the gentle, contemplative sunset phase of my broken-field scramble through life. Being young was exciting, but it was never as comfortable as this. I enjoy the sunsets. Hone my hammock technique. Smell the proverbial roses. Call me a quitter, but when I'm ninety-three I don't particularly want to be rigged out in a bionic exoskeleton to chase tennis balls.

Or baseballs. Somebody once asked Joe DiMaggio how he knew when it was time to hang up his cleats.

"I was standing at the plate," said Joe. "The pitcher threw the ball and my brain said, 'Swing!' And my body said, 'Who, me?'"

Good enough for the Yankee Clipper. Good enough for me.

Anyone for Finger Food?

Customer: Waiter! What's this fly doing in my soup?
Waiter: Hmm. Looks like the backstroke, sir.

A ll corny joking aside, put yourself in Denny Lynch's Hush
Puppies. You're a young management type living in San Jose,
California, and by and large, your personal universe is unfolding as
it should. You're happily married. Your car starts every time you turn
the ignition key. The restaurant you operate—a Wendy's outlet—is a
popular one. You're full up most nights with lots of enthusiastic reg-
ulars. More than a few of them even make a point of coming up to
the cash register and telling you how much they liked their meals.

Then comes the evening of March 22, 2005. A woman at table
thirteen is causing a ruckus. She demands to see the manager. Well,
it happens. Sometimes a burger is underdone or the coleslaw is missing. Occasionally the coffee is lukewarm instead of piping hot.

But it's different this time. The woman is white-faced and she is
coughing and retching and pointing disgustedly towards her unfin-
ished bowl of Wendy's chili. More specifically she is pointing at a
brownish, eraser-sized morsel sitting on the plate beside her chili
bowl.

It looks like it could be a chunk of meat or maybe a sprig of
celery, except for one thing.

It has a long, manicured fingernail attached to it. It's a portion of a severed human finger. And the customer is claiming that she found it the hard way—by chomping into it.

Oh, and she says one other thing, between her gasps for breath. She says she's suing.

And sue she does. Anna Ayala, aged thirty-nine, of Las Vegas, hires herself a lawyer and files a multimillion-dollar claim against JEM Management Group, which owns the Wendy's franchise where she ate.

Naturally the story goes global. There's something about tales of body parts in fast food that tickles the morbid funny bone of news reporters. Letterman and Leno crack wise about it. Anna Ayala's story becomes the humorous ending "kicker" for newscasts all over the planet.

And at Wendy's, they're in full damage control. They call in the cops, who grill every Wendy's employee who possibly could have slipped the digit into the chow. They give the whole staff Voice Stress Analysis tests to discover if any of them are lying. They hire a fleet of private investigators to track down the person who used to be attached to the finger. They trace all their chili ingredients back to their suppliers to see if anybody along the way suffered a serious hand injury. Wendy's also offers a fifty-thousand-dollar reward for information about the origin of the finger. Just hours later they double the award to one hundred thousand dollars.

Meanwhile it's as if a stink bomb has gone off, not just in the outlet where Anna Ayala dined on that fateful March night, but at Wendy's outlets all over California. Customers are staying away in droves. Wendy's starts reducing shifts and even laying off employees.

But then some curious facts emerge.

Investigators determine that the severed finger at the centre of the mystery was "fresh," so to speak, not cooked. In other words, it didn't come with the chili. It was planted.

And then the San Jose police discover that Ms. Ayala is no stranger to lawsuits against large corporations. She had previously sued General Motors, Goodyear Tire and El Pollo Loco, another restaurant chain.

Anna Ayala is, in short, a fraud and a phony. Her lawsuit is kaput, and instead of moving up to Park Place, she has gone Directly To Jail.

The upshot of her little scam? Fast Food Chill. Wendy's restaurants in California shoulder losses in the millions of dollars and scores of Wendy's employees are looking for work. Wendy's customers are straggling back slowly, but nobody's ordering chili.

On the upside, Anna Ayala is sitting in a San Jose jail cell awaiting a date with a judge.

Here's hoping the judge gives her the finger.

Hey You! Yeah,
I'm Talking to You!

Ever get the feeling that the whole world is out to make you paranoid? It's not you, pal, it's life. And anyway, you're not as paranoid as Scott Stevens—yet. Mr. Stevens used to be the weather guy on KPVI-TV in Pocatello, Idaho, but no longer. Not that he was bad at the job. He was fine. But he wanted more time to pursue and prove his personal conviction—that the viciousness of Hurricane Katrina was caused by a Russian-made electromagnetic generator employed by the fiendish Japanese mafia known as Yakuza.

Stevens figures it's all about revenge for the World War II bombing of Hiroshima and Nagasaki. "The patterns and odd geometric shapes in the sky are unmistakable evidence," he says, "that our weather is being stolen from us."

Austin Powers, where are you when we need you?

Speaking of Ms. Katrina, we can thank her for the fact that armed dolphins are now on the loose somewhere in the Gulf of Mexico.

I am not making this up.

According to a report in Britain's *Observer,* military experts in the US Navy have trained dolphins to "shoot terrorists and pinpoint spies underwater." These Atlantic bottlenose dolphins—there are thirty-six of them—are kitted out with toxic dart guns.

Their compound on the Louisiana coast was flooded during Hurricane Katrina and the dolphins disappeared, presumably into the gulf, where they are no doubt milling around like boyz from the 'hood, packing heat and looking for action.

How does a bottlenose dolphin differentiate between an Al Qaeda suicide bomber aquanaut and oh, say, a pudgy Canuck vacationer in flowered shorts, snorkel and swim fins?

Dolphins are smart, but they're not *that* smart. Which is why I won't be dabbling my tootsies in the Gulf of Mexico anytime soon.

On the up-side of the paranoia sweepstakes, the market for Elvis-is-alive-and-pumping-gas-in-Wichita wagers has virtually dried up. British bookmakers quoted by England's ITV confirmed that betting action on whether The King was still alive and hiding out somewhere "has almost completely disappeared."

"It is perhaps," said London bookie Rupert Adams somewhat grandly, "the end of an era."

Perhaps—and maybe just as well. If Elvis were alive he'd be seventy-one come January—and if he was still horsing down the fried peanut butter and banana sandwiches the way he was when he "disappeared" in 1977, he would weigh approximately five hundred kilograms.

And now for the paranoia *pièce de résistance.* We have discovered—at last—the true whereabouts of the Weapons of Mass Distraction the Americans have been looking for. They—it, actually—has been found within the very bosom of the Bush family.

Did I mention I'm not making any of this up?

At a ceremony naming the new speaker of the state legislature, Dubya's brother, Florida governor Jeb Bush, decided that the time was ripe to reveal the royal jelly in the Bush family closet. It's a chap by the name of Chang.

"Chang is a mystical warrior," Governor Bush told the assembled crowd. "Chang is somebody who believes in conservative principles, believes in entrepreneurial capitalism, believes in moral values that underpin a free society . . . I rely on Chang with great regularity in my public life. He has been by my side and sometimes I let him down. But Chang, this mystical warrior, has never let me down."

Turns out that Jeb learned all about Chang at his daddy's knee. George Herbert Bush believed in Chang too. Bush *père* was famous for muttering "unleash Chang" to himself when facing a troublesome tennis opponent. He also invoked Chang whenever he wanted people to stop arguing with him.

There's no indication that the Bush currently ensconced in the Oval Office—Bush Lite, as it were—kneels at the alter of Chang. Dubya's more inclined to worship Ching.

You know—that sound a Halliburton cash register makes?

Extreme Tourism

When I was a kid, we didn't have tourists. We had visitors. Like Uncle Mike and Aunt Dolores, who showed up every summer and took over the spare bedroom. They never did any touristy things, sightseeing or taking pictures or writing post cards or such. Uncle Mike slept a lot and Aunt D. just fanned herself and sighed and complained about the heat. They showed up for meals, made small talk in the living room and drank up most of Dad's homemade beer. Then one day they packed up and went home. That's as close as we got to tourists.

But then tourism became big business. Suddenly there were "tourist destinations" like Cancun and Disneyworld, Vegas and Whistler.

Got big locally too.

Tourism is huge on Salt Spring, where I live. We don't have any casinos or Céline Dion concerts but I counted over eighty bed and breakfasts in the phone book before my eyes crossed. And lots more don't even bother to advertise.

But bed and breakfasts, casinos and cruise ships—they all have one thing in common. It's nanny tourism. Lots of pampering involved. Margaritas by the pool, massages on the afterdeck, blueberry scones with your morning tea. Very nice for the indolent and unmotivated, who just want to veg out and be catered to—but not challenging enough for some travellers.

For them, there's adventure tourism. Mountain biking, rock climbing, hang gliding, whitewater rafting—stuff that calls for physical commitment along with your Visa card number and expiry date.

Still, even that can seem kinda . . . self-indulgent. Which is why adventure tourism gave birth to another energetic offspring. One that came with brownie points—kayaking with orcas in the Inside Passage, howling with wolves in the Kootenays, swimming with salmon at Campbell River, grizzly watching in the Great Bear Rainforest—lo, was born the concept of ecotourism.

Well folks, it's time for another mighty morph. Ecotourism begets . . . wacko tourism. Tourism above and beyond the call of common sense. Or even sanity.

Exhibit A: Dennis Tito, the sixty-year-old California gazillion-aire who spent twenty million US dollars to hitch a ride with Russia's Federal Space Agency and become the first tourist in space.

Exhibit B: The Vancouver Island schnooks who got taken for a ride by West Coast tour guide Dave Martin recently. You hear about that? Fifty people paid a hundred bucks each for the privilege of hiking a horrendous trek in the mountains of Strathcona Park hoping to qualify for a spot on a Canadian version of the TV show *Survivor.* The supposedly three-hour trek turned out to be more like twenty hours. There were no maps, no safety crew, no provisions and no sanction from authorities. Twenty-three participants had to be airlifted out by search and rescue helicopters.

Ah well. Could've been even wackier. Could have been Steve Currey in charge. Steve was an explorer with an even more adventur-ous expedition in the works. If you have free time and twenty-five thousand bucks burning a hole in your Tilley shorts, you can sign up for a cruise on a Russian nuclear icebreaker and go in search of the Arctic entrance to the centre of the earth. It's hollow, you know. Before he died, Steve promised that expedition members would meet up with the legendary Lost Tribes of Israel down there. (They migrated to the centre of the earth back in 687 BC, said Steve.) The

Currey Expeditions brochure promised you'd also get to ride an inner earth monorail to the Lost Garden of Eden, and break bread with the great High Priest of the Inner World, who happens to be a direct descendant of King David.

You think I sound like I stumbled face-first into a Salt Spring grow op? Think again—and check it out for yourself at www.ourhollowearth.com.

But hey—if the North Pole is too remote and twenty-five grand is too rich for your blood, drop *me* a line.

For fifty bucks I'll take you up to the hidden valley on Mount Belcher where you can see the crop circles left by the flying saucers the Sasquatch took off in just before the CIA's black helicopters came in to fake that documentary about the so-called moon landing.

It'll be great. I'll even treat you to a homemade beer. Still got my dad's recipe.

Wretched Excess

Recently a dark blue monster ploughed inexorably through the BC coastal waters. It was spotted several times in English Bay just off Vancouver. It was also seen gliding ghostlike across the Strait of Georgia and threading its way through the waters around the Gulf Islands.

And I do mean monster. This nautical apparition is seven storeys high and longer than a football field, and it can move faster than a great white shark all day long. *Le Grand Bleu* (Big Blue), the fifth largest private yacht in the world, belongs to Russian billionaire Roman Abramovich, who is officially the twenty-first richest man in the world.

Conspicuous consumption? Well, I guess. *Le Grand Bleu* boasts a crew of fifty and deck accessories that include an eighteen-metre motor launch, a twenty-two-metre sailboat and oh yes—a helicopter. And did I mention the submarine? Yes, an on-deck submarine.

And then there's Philip Green, of London, England, sixty-seventh richest person in the world. Mr. Green is, among other things, gazillionaire owner of the British Home Stores retail chain. Recently he planned a bar mitzvah for his young son. Most dads might shell out for a catered evening in a hotel suite or perhaps a large party-type tent for the backyard. Green ordered an entire custom-built synagogue. To be erected on the French Riviera. Oh, and entertainment, of course. He'd fly in Justin Timberlake to lip synch a couple of ballads for his boy. Justin would pick up a million bucks for the gig.

Wretched excess—it's everywhere. Lee Kun-hee runs the giant Samsung electronics company out of South Korea. With a bankroll of a mere 4.3 billion dollars, Mr. Lee is doomed to a dismal 126th slot on the richest-people-in-the-world list, but he's not just a working stiff.

This tycoon likes to kick back and relax now and again. In particular Mr. Lee likes to downhill ski in his off time, but he doesn't care for those pesky crowds and annoying lineups that skiers like you and me have to endure on the slopes of Whistler, Big White or Mont Tremblant.

Mr. Lee has found a solution to this tiresome problem of overcrowding. The Samsung chief rents his own Alp. Three entire mountain slopes at fashionable Courchevel in the French Alps. Having two mountainside hectares netted off protects Mr. Lee from the vulgar common schussers and allows him to concentrate on the lessons he receives from his six full-time ski instructors.

The rich, eh? F. Scott Fitzgerald once said to Hemingway, "The rich are different from you and me." To which Hemingway replied, "Yes. They have more money." Well, Ernie was an outdoorsy kind of guy. I wonder what he'd have made of Christopher Ott of Naples, Florida.

Mr. Ott is a big game hunter. Big time. A couple of years ago he bought a special hunting tag from the BC government that allowed him to bag one Rocky Mountain sheep. But this was a special hunting tag. When he went after his prey (with a government-certified guide), Mr. Ott could jump the official BC hunting season by anywhere up to three weeks. Which means he would be the only hunter on the mountain. Clearly membership in this exclusive club of one had its privileges, but the admission charge was pretty steep. Christopher Ott paid 180 thousand Canadian dollars for that hunting tag. And that's not cheap as sheep shots go.

Jealous? Why should I be jealous? I don't envy Mr. Ott his

luxury safari, nor Phil Green his impending pleasure palace on the French Riviera. And I am not green about Roman Abramovich's yacht *Le Grande Bleu* either.

I've got my own boat. It's as long as, well, a ping pong table. Deck accessories include two life jackets, a baling can and matching oarlocks. But that's okay. I'm a minimalist kind of guy.

Which is a good thing to be, considering my failure to even register as an also-ran on the rich guys' list. I'm with Henny Youngman, who said, "I've got all the money I'll ever need. Providing I die by four o'clock."

Some other wise guy once said, "Better to live rich than to die rich."

That's what I'm working on.